Brunswick

The Story of an American Company
from 1845 to 1985

Rick Kogan

Brunswick Corporation, One Brunswick Plaza, Skokie, Illinois 60077

Acknowledgements

My aim in these pages was not only to trace the history of the Brunswick Corporation but to convey its flavor and tone at specific periods during its remarkable lifetime. If I have succeeded it was with the help of many people. It would be impossible in this space to thank them all. Nevertheless, I am especially indebted to the dozens of former Brunswick executives, employees and family members who shared with me their memories and mementos; the helpful staffs of the Chicago Public Library, the Municipal Reference Library, library of the Chicago Historical Society, and the "morgues" of the Chicago Sun-Times and Chicago Tribune; Diana Haskell and Ed Meachen of the Newberry Library, Frances Forman of the Cincinnati Historical Society, Fannie Zelcer of the American Jewish Archives, and Ann Riker at the University of Illinois; a number of writers and reporters whose past words about Brunswick were of incalculable aid; "William Hendricks' History of Billiards," and the more contemporary "Billiards" by John Grissim for their entertaining and informative looks at billiards' formative years; and a most profound thanks to the current executives and employees of the Brunswick Corporation around the globe who gave of their time and energy to help shape this book in which all of them share.

Rick Kogan
August, 1985

About the Author

Chicago journalist Rick Kogan has been a reporter, editor and columnist for all of Chicago's major daily newspapers, the *Daily News, Sun-Times* and *Tribune.*

A native Chicagoan, he is the author of *Yesterday's Chicago,* in collaboration with Herman Kogan, *Dr. Night Life's Chicago,* a collection of columns, and *Sabers & Suites,* a history of Chicago's Ambassador East Hotel. In the summer of 1984, he was commissioned by the Brunswick Corporation to write its corporate history.

Contents

1 *Brunswick*

Through the years, the company started by John Brunswick has had many names. But to the public, it has always been Brunswick, a name that stands for quality.

The name is synonymous in the American consciousness with bowling and billiards. However, walking through the lobby of the company's corporate headquarters north of Chicago, one would discover a surprisingly vast array of products no less important in establishing the heritage of this 140-year-old company. From products for marine power, defense and aerospace, energy, transportation, and recreation, the story of Brunswick is one of risks and challenges—played out against a backdrop of a century and a half of social, economic, and technological change.

There are but a few American businesses that date as far back into America's history as does Brunswick. A long corporate life is filled with challenges—the unpredictable nature of the economy, the public's capricious tastes, changing leadership. While other companies have vanished, Brunswick remains. The reasons for its survival and its continued success are complex, a combination of many elements that form a rich and unique portrait of corporate life.

There are thousands of people who have played a part in this story—from the now-nameless workmen who helped John Brunswick make his first billiard tables in 1845, to Michael J. "Dad" Whalen who invented a rubber bowling ball, to Ernest Hedenskoog who worked for 40 years trying to build an automatic pin-setting machine, to E. C. Kiekhaefer who transformed a broken-down outboard motor company into Mercury Marine, to the 19,000 employees around the world today.

There is no precise way to gauge the contributions of the company's many employees, past and present. One must inevitably look at the men in charge, for the company mirrors their personality and character. For most of its existence, Brunswick was a family concern, owned throughout the 19th century almost entirely by the Brunswick and Bensinger families. In the 20th century, as the company's stock began to be dispersed into the hands of various descendants and to others through public offerings, the family relinquished its voting control of the corporation. Nevertheless, for its key management, the company was led until 1966 by members of the Bensinger family. Remarkably, during Brunswick's 140 years it has had only nine leaders.

When John Brunswick set out to make his first billiard table in a musty second-floor workshop in Cincinnati he had a simple goal: To make the best billiard table in the world.

Thus was born a corporate philosophy that continues to guide the company today. Brunswick's concerns for quality and craftsmanship formed the iron-firm basis upon which all those who followed could build. And build they did.

Brunswick's son-in-law Moses Bensinger successfully moved the firm into the bowling and bar furnishings areas. His son Benjamin's entrepreneurial spirit brought the company into such new areas as automobile tires, phonographs, and records. In all of these fields, only the best would do. "My father was not happy making any except the finest quality goods," Benjamin Bensinger said of his father Moses. Indeed, this philosophy propelled the company through most of its first century and enabled Benjamin's son Bob to steer the company successfully through the ravages of the Depression.

The nature of the company began to change dramatically in the 1950s, when the incredible success of the company's Automatic Pinsetter enabled Bob Bensinger's brother, Ted, to acquire 18 companies including Mercury and Zebco. Almost overnight he transformed Brunswick into a diversified company.

With that growth came problems that eventually needed outside help. Jack L. Hanigan remedied the company's financial ills and began to provide balanced growth for the company by concentrating on burgeoning medical and technical fields, including the homegrown defense division. His successor, K. Brooks Abernathy, continued that pattern, solidifying the company's position in new markets.

In 1982, Brunswick was rocked by a bitter takeover battle. To remain intact it was forced to dispose of its lucrative medical business. Under Jack Reichert, who took over at that time, the company, in his words, began to "focus on present businesses and not try to be something we aren't."

Relying on values that had characterized Brunswick's long history—a bent toward entrepreneurship and innovation; a commitment to individuality framed within corporate goals; and an abiding concern for quality, close ties between company and customers, employees' sense of identification with the products, and management's concern for the long run—Reichert brought Brunswick boldly into a new, exciting era.

In each of the many markets the company served, Reichert demanded one thing: To be the best. And that is something John Brunswick would understand.

The Many Names of Brunswick

1845
John M. Brunswick

1858
J.M. Brunswick & Bro.

1866
J.M. Brunswick & Bros.

1871
J.M. Brunswick & Bro.

1872
J.M. Brunswick Billiard Mfg. Co.

1874
J.M. Brunswick & Balke Co.

1884
Brunswick Balke Collender Co.

1960
Brunswick Corp.

2 *Planting the Seeds*

John Brunswick comes to America where he builds his own small company into the world's largest billiard equipment firm

Before his 15th birthday, John Brunswick traded the peace and quiet of his hometown Bremgarten in the Rhine Valley to embark on an arduous and lengthy journey that would take him to an unknown future and certain adventure in the wilds of America.

The picturesque city of Bremgarten is a minor tourist attraction of Switzerland's Rhine valley. It is a place where change comes slowly, and guidebooks often point out its 11th Century bridge, which sits above the River Reuss near the center of town.

This is where a young mother died giving birth to her first child, John Moses Brunswick, on October 16, 1819. The child's father, Benedict, raised the dark-haired boy alone for two years, until he remarried and began another family.

Throughout his life, John Brunswick rarely talked about his childhood. His parents were Jewish and his nationality, since Bremgarten shared more characteristics with its northern neighbor than its own country, more German than Swiss. By all indications, his father was a kind man, but it is nevertheless likely that the boy felt increasingly like a stranger in his father's new family.

From travellers passing through town, he heard stories of America, compelling tales of a wild place across the Atlantic. It was not the land of opportunity that would inspire the immigrant waves of the late 1800s. Whatever stories young John Brunswick heard were not of

Brunswick spent his first months in America dodging vehicles such as this one on the streets of New York. An observant young man, he determined that a prosperous future lay in the carriage-making industry and set about to fashion a career.

The sea voyage to America was long; and the discomfort, extreme. Grateful even to be alive, Brunswick huddled with other immigrants upon arrival in New York. Like them, he carried little more than some meager provisions and a few big dreams.

streets paved with gold but of a raw country of barely beaten paths.

It pulled him, though, away from the quiet of Bremgarten shortly before his fifteenth birthday, a sack of clothes across his back and a few coins in his pocket.

On foot he travelled to nearby Basel where he took a train, bounce after bone-jarring bounce, across Germany to the bustling North Sea port of Bremen. There he spent hours haggling over his fare. Shipping companies, which brought tobacco, cotton, and grain to Europe, had just begun returning to America freighted with emigrants. Sea captains and brokers shouted their deals from the pier, and some pressed crudely made

guidebooks into young Brunswick's hands.

The voyage by ship was long and the discomfort extreme. Brunswick was herded together with other emigrants and slept on a floor sparsely covered with sawdust. He carried his own meager provisions, for none were available on ship. He ate them cold, listening to the other passengers share their dreams and fears.

Some 40 days after setting sail, his ship arrived in New York's Manhattan harbor. There was no Statue of Liberty to greet Brunswick—she was more than 50 years away. On a warm late summer day in 1834, Brunswick stepped gingerly into America's largest city.

His first days in the city were confusing, but he was able to find work as an errand boy for a German butcher in the Wall Street area. The pace of the city was frantic, at once ominous and exhilarating. Day after day, Brunswick ran along the narrow and winding streets of the city, delivering packages to wooden cottage houses and brick buildings an amazing four or five stories high. He fought his way through packs of newspaper vendors, chimney sweeps, secondhand-clothes salesmen, itinerant repairmen, and strawberry vendors as they vied in shouting each other down. Gas lamps lit his darkness at the end of a day's work, and he returned to his rooming house exhausted.

Six months of that life was enough. How could he observe

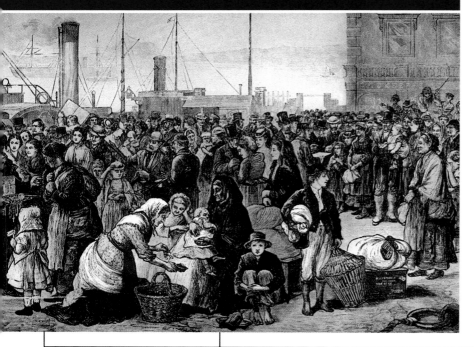

life's possibilities amid Manhattan's frenzy? Carrying his belongings in a small bag, he took a train to Philadelphia. In less than a week, he found work with a carriage maker.

It was the job he wanted. In New York he had seen, and spent a good portion of each day dodging, the astonishing number of vehicles that raced along the streets. Among these were the clarence and rockaway, the landau and landaulet, the open coupe, the barouche, the phaeton for speed lovers, and the double tandem mail coach. The carriage-making industry was flourishing. In Philadelphia, it had begun humbly in a wheelwright's shop a few years before the Revolution. When Bruns-

wick arrived, the local carriage-making business was prosperous and growing.

And how much better Philadelphia suited Brunswick. It was an austere place full of dark colors and rectangular avenues which were completely deserted after 10 o'clock at night. Charles Dickens commented, after walking the city's streets, that he would "give anything for a winding road."

Brunswick spent four quiet years in Philadelphia as an apprentice carriage maker, finally leaving for nearby Harrisburg and a position as journeyman with a German firm owned by a man named Greiner. Greiner's daughter, 17-year-old Louisa, spent an increasing amount of time at the

This view of Central Street shows the peaceful nature of Philadelphia during the four years Brunswick spent there learning to make carriages.

Running errands for a German butcher, Brunswick found New York's streets clogged with carriages of all shapes, sizes, and purposes, as was this stretch of Old Broadway in the 1830s.

Coughing dark smoke into the valley air, steamboats line Cincinnati's docks— a vivid example of the city's prosperity in the 1830s.

shop, talking with Brunswick. Within seven months the two were married.

Brunswick moved into the Greiner house and continued to work for his father-in-law. His future seemed clear. When Greiner retired, his lucrative business would become Brunswick's. Clear perhaps, but too easy for Brunswick. He had not come to America to follow in another's footsteps.

In 1840 he and his wife moved to Cincinnati. Not only was it the most prosperous town in the west, it had a large German community in which the young couple would feel at home. During the 1830s, more than 30,000 Germans had moved to Cincinnati. The Miami Canal became their Rhine, and the place where the Germans lived was "Over the Rhine."

A writer at the time captured the scene: "One has no sooner entered the northern districts of the city lying beyond Court Street across the canal, than he finds himself in a foreign atmosphere— a foreign land. The people are Germans; their very gossip is German."

The city's principal industry was meat packing. So many stray pigs wandered the streets of the downtown area that the city was derisively but profitably called "Porkopolis." The waters of Deer Creek ran red with blood from slaughter-

houses, and visitors marveled that carriages stopped to permit pigs to be herded across the street.

Some of those carriages were the handiwork of Brunswick, who was employed as a journeyman at a number of Cincinnati firms, including Bruce Brothers, Lawyer & Company, and Fulton Omnibus. When the latter company went out of business in 1841, as an unprecedented economic depression hit the country, Brunswick found himself out of work. Unable to latch on with another carriage-making company, he was finally forced to take a job as a steward on a river steamboat.

It was obvious to Brunswick that river commerce was immune to the depression. Along the Cincinnati riverfront, steamboats were often tied bow to stern for more than six miles, coughing thick black smoke into the fresh valley air. The system of inland canals branching out from the Ohio River had opened up the heartland, enabling farmers to move their products to the river for shipping to southern markets.

Steamboats stopped frequently along the Ohio and Mississippi to take on or put off freight. This river trading was commerce at its most fundamental, and it amazed such travellers as the poet Walt Whitman, who wrote: "At one place . . . we shipped several hundred barrels of pork; ditto of lard; at another place, an uncounted lot of flour . . . besides bags of coffee, rolls of leather, groceries, dry goods, hardware, all sorts of agricultural products, innumerable coops filled with live geese, turkeys, and fowls."

Brunswick could not resist. With what few extra dollars he could gather, he plunged into the trading. Though barely 22-years-old, he did well against older, more experienced traders. He was a tough haggler and surprisingly prescient in buy low/sell high commerce. He loved this new life, and he prospered. His health, however, could not withstand the rough-and-tumble river pace. Pneumonia forced him off the river and into bed for nearly five months. Once he recovered, his desire to return to the river was thwarted by his wife's pleas and his own fear of

Forced from the carriage-making trade by an economic depression, Brunswick took work as a steward on a riverboat that plied the Ohio River. He soon started trading goods and proved a natural. When he left the river, he had enough money to open his own woodworking shop.

Using crude tools such as the ones below, Brunswick and his employees worked long hours in his cramped and dusty shop making a wide variety of products—not only carriages, but cabinets and chairs, as well.

a relapse. He took the money accumulated from trading, rented a small workshop, and began his own carriage-making company.

The depression had eased by 1845, and competition in the carriage-making business was more intense than ever. Brunswick worked tirelessly, and hired only those men willing to match his long hours. He was demanding but fair, seeking the highest quality in the design and practicality of his products. Business went well. He moved to larger quarters and hired more woodsmiths. If there were no carriages to be built, Brunswick and his workmen made other items, including chairs, tables and cabinets.

"If it is wood, we can make it," Brunswick would tell his employ-

ees. "And we can make it better than anyone else."

As his business increased, so did his reputation in the community. Socially, the self-made man was the hero of the day, embodying the highly respected qualities of courage, imagination, ingenuity, and self-confidence.

Brunswick became increasingly involved with local political, religious, and social groups. He was an active supporter of many Jewish organizations, spent many nights talking business at men's clubs, and began attending social events at the homes of other prominent businessmen.

At one such party, a lavish dinner gathering in 1845, the host took Brunswick aside and led him

to a large room. In the middle stood a billiard table.

"This is a Thurston Superior," the host said proudly. "It's from England. Same fellow made a table for Napoleon. It's a fine table, isn't it? Feel the woodwork. . . . John, what do you think of it? Fine craftsmanship, no?"

Brunswick did not answer. He was transfixed, and for many minutes rubbed his hands along the finely carved wood of the table like a sculptor carefully examining a rival's work.

The first references to billiards in this country have little to do with the pastime. Tables were used for a variety of unsportsmanlike activities. They frequently functioned as everything from banquet tables and temporary morgues, to guest beds for up to six at a time, and operating tables. Paralleling billiards' earlier history in Europe, the game gradually found its way out of the homes of the upper classes and into taverns all along the colonial seaboard, where in a short time it became associated with drinking and gambling.

Puritans railed against the game. Still, George Washington played, and John Quincy Adams had a billiard table installed in the White House at his own expense, giving his congressional critics a chance to raise hell over his acquisition of "gambling furniture."

Though this image problem has dogged billiards to this day, there was another reason for the game's early limited popularity: crude playing equipment. It was a frustrating game, nearly impossible to master. Cue sticks were nothing more than tapered poles of ash or maple without leather tips. Table cushions were imperfect, consisting of cloth sleeves stuffed with

Early billiard equipment was crude and unreliable; nevertheless, this group gathered to do battle, and invite frustration, over a Virginia tavern billiard table in the early 1800s.

11

cotton, sawdust, feathers, or strips of felt. Table beds were made of warp-prone wood.

But in the decades preceding Brunswick's entry into the billiard business, a number of remarkable technical innovations began to transform the game.

● John Thurston, the most prominent billiard table manufacturer in England, had long searched for a proper cushion material. He experimented with horsehair, swanskin, Russian duck feathers, and even human hair. The results of those experiments were unimpressive, but Thurston found success in another facet of the game when, in 1826, he adopted a thick, warp-resistant slate bedding for his tables.

● A French infantry captain named Mingaud, jailed for unlawful political activity, whiled away his sentence playing billiards in prison. To soften the harshness of his stroke, and thereby cut down on miscues, Mingaud glued a piece of leather to the tip of his cue. He discovered that by striking the ball slightly off center, it could be made to do an astonishing number of things. He experimented for months, trying to understand his discovery. When his prison term expired, he demanded, and was granted, another month in jail so he could further investigate what became known as cue ball english.

● In 1835, the first crude rubber from India was substituted for cloth in table cushions. In the 1840s, it was discovered that by melting the rubber at different temperatures and mixing it with sulphur compounds, its elasticity could be increased and precisely controlled, its durability could be prolonged, and the problematic effects of temperature and humidity variations all but eliminated.

The advent of this better equipment and materials was a boon to Brunswick and other early billiard manufacturers, coinciding with America's emergence from non-athletic times. Until the 1840s, Americans had a distinct aversion to sports and exercise. The growth of popular sporting activities and events resulted from the growth of cities and the easing of living conditions. Before that time, it had been an academic question. It is hard to imagine a prairie settler, exhausted by daylong physical labor, enjoying sports in his leisure.

The range of sports in antebellum America was narrow. Baseball and football were not widely known before 1850. The principal spectator sports in cities were horse trotting, professional footraces, and competitive rowing. But billiards was coming on strong. Indeed, one of the major pre-Civil War sporting events was the first National Billiard Championship in Detroit in 1859, a match between Michael Phelan and John Seereiter.

Phelan's participation assured a big crowd. He was well known as a reputable manufacturer; two years before, he had patented a combination cushion that set new standards for tables. He was also an expert player, the author of two books on the game, owner of a billiard parlor in New York, and billiard columnist for several major newspapers.

Phelan and Seereiter met over four days in April, playing for an extravagant $15,000 purse. On the final night, more than 400 fans paid five dollars a head for seats in the gallery. Outside, another 4,000 people cheered as results were announced through a megaphone. Journalists from a dozen dailies filled the makeshift pressbox. Magazine illustrators scribbled on sketchpads.

Phelan and Seereiter, wearing vests and long-sleeved shirts, played brilliantly, each scoring as many as 50 points an inning. The lead seesawed back and forth. Just before dawn, Phelan stepped to the table leading 1,954 to 1,904. He ran the next 46 balls, winning the contest.

As this dramatic 1863 illustration shows, even the Civil War did not dampen billiards' growing popularity. This match, held in June in New York, attracted huge crowds. Michael Phelan was eliminated early, and the championship was eventually captured by Dudley Kavanaugh, here shown lining up a shot during the finals.

This replica of one of Brunswick's earliest billiard tables speaks eloquently for its art and craftsmanship. Incorporating the latest technological advances, the table helped to popularize the game, quickly propelling Brunswick's company into leadership in the burgeoning industry.

John Brunswick produced his first billiard table in the autumn of 1845. As he and his craftsmen constructed the table, Brunswick had no hint of the game's potential. He was guided by an entrepreneurial spirit. Like the cabinets, tables, chairs, and carriages he was also making, the billiard table was another wooden item—an experiment in wood for which he hoped to create a market.

He did. His first billiard table customer, a successful local meat-packer, was so pleased with his purchase that he became a vociferous booster of Brunswick tables. One by one, other prominent citizens walked into Brunswick's workshop and ordered their own tables.

Within two years, orders for tables were arriving from cities as far away as Chicago and New Orleans. From the outset, Brunswick's tables were paragons of the woodworker's skill, eye-catching blends of function and form. Some of these early tables are outrageously ornate by today's standards, but the best of them, without stretching a point, can be called works of art.

For all of his appreciation for and understanding of aesthetics, however, it was Brunswick's business acumen that was primarily responsible for the company's early success. Sensing the need for expansion, Brunswick sent for his

half-brothers from Switzerland. As early as 1848, half-brothers David and Emanuel had established a sales office for him on State Street in Chicago. This branch quickly expanded to include a small factory and 8,000-square-foot billiard parlor on Washington Street, and a large factory on State Street. In 1852, a sales office was established in New Orleans, and in 1859 a salesroom and billiard hall were opened in St. Louis. Half-brothers Joseph and Hyman worked at the company's headquarters in Cincinnati.

All of the half-brothers played important roles in an aggressive business strategy. During the 1850s and 1860s, the Brunswicks engaged in vigorous competition with a number of smaller manufacturers. In addition, the company bought out suppliers of such raw materials as quarried slate and hardwood timber.

In 1858, the company was operating as J. M. Brunswick & Brother (half-brother Joseph). The following year, in a pamphlet called "Cincinnati in 1859," the company received the following profile: "J. M. Brunswick & Brother, salesroom and warehouse, No. 8 west Sixth street, manufacture annually, to the value of two hundred thousand dollars, of these tables. They work seventy-five

hands, and furnish equipment of every article in this line. Their tables are of the first quality and finish."

The company name changed slightly in 1866, to J. M. Brunswick & Brothers, when half-brother Emanuel was also listed as a principal. By 1869, when a song called "Billiards on the Brain" accurately captured the game's popularity, the fight for the biggest share of the billiard market was down to a three-company battle. Brunswick, along with son-in-law Moses Bensinger, who had recently joined the firm, vied with Julius Balke's Great Western Billiard Manufactory of Cincinnati for the burgeoning western market, and with Phelan & Collender of New York, which dominated the east.

A pair of ads (above) in an 1859 Cincinnati directory captures the rivalry between that city's two leading billiard manufacturers. It wasn't long, however, before Brunswick and Balke joined forces and started producing such lavish tables as the Monarch, trumpeted in such imposing ads as the one below.

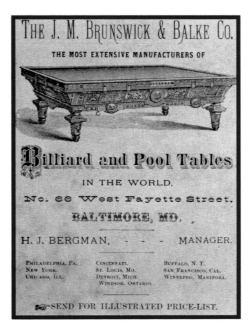

3 *Back Bars and Bowling*

Brunswick's son-in-law, Moses Bensinger, propels the company into eventual dominance in the bowling and bar businesses

Lavish and detailed illustrations highlighted the Brunswick catalogue before the turn of the century as the company was selling almost as many billiard tables as it could make. And amid this prosperity the company's attention was grabbed by the potential of a sport called bowling.

Moses Bensinger had surprised many of his friends when he announced in 1867 that he would marry Eleanora Brunswick, the pleasant daughter of John and Louisa Brunswick. He further surprised those who knew him when he did not rush immediately to join his father-in-law's thriving billiard business, choosing to remain in Louisville and continue to work as an apprentice to a jewelry maker.

Bensinger's spirit of independence obviously appealed to John Brunswick. He talked occasionally with Moses about business, often after holiday celebrations at Brunswick's Cincinnati home. But it was not until 1869, shortly after Moses and Eleanora presented

him with a lively grandson they named Benjamin, that Brunswick employed his considerable sales skills to bring Moses into the family firm.

The battle with Balke and Phelan & Collender was intense and demanded more energy than Brunswick was able to muster. He had footsoldiers aplenty—the employees in his expanding company—but he lacked a trusted aide to lead his troops.

It will never be known what qualities Brunswick found lacking in his other three sons-in-law, but in Moses Bensinger he sensed some of his own ambition, intelligence, and business fortitude. Tragically, two of his own sons had died during the 1860s. Louis

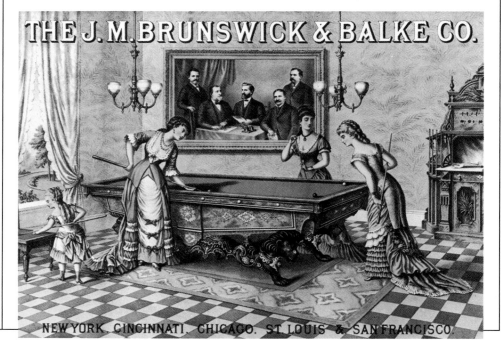

THE J. M. BRUNSWICK & BALKE CO.

NEW YORK. CINCINNATI. CHICAGO. ST. LOUIS & SAN FRANCISCO.

Moses Bensinger, playfully posed with his wife Eleanora, would be proud to know that Brunswick bars made in the 1880s are still in use today. This striking model is the focal point of a popular Chicago restaurant.

Brunswick was a handsome 16-year-old when he drowned in the muddy waters of the Licking River, and Harry was barely 21 when he was trapped aboard a ferryboat as it burned after colliding with a barge on the Ohio River. His youngest child, Benedict Henry, born in 1860, was too young to become involved in business.

Brunswick relied increasingly on Moses Bensinger, who began as a salesman. In 1872, when the company was reorganized as the J. M. Brunswick Billiard Manufacturing Company, Bensinger was made a vice president, as were two long-time employees, A. F. Troescher and Leo Schmidt.

It was Bensinger who was the principal architect of the 1873 merger with Julius Balke's firm. The company name was changed to the J. M. Brunswick & Balke Company, and it was incorporated with a capital stock of $275,000.

During this period Brunswick was having considerable problems with his ambitious half-brothers. Especially troublesome appears to have been Emanuel, who started a rival billiard firm in Chicago. Pre-Chicago Fire records are virtually nonexistent, but a pamphlet published two years after the fire, in 1873, captures what seems to have been a heated battle between half-brothers:

"THE J.M. BRUNSWICK & BALKE COMPANY—Billiard-table Manufactory—62 Lake Street—was established in 1848, and is the oldest house in the Northwest; capital investment, $200,000; number of employees, 60; weekly payroll, $900; annual production, 700 tables, valued at $400,000. This company has furnished tables for Foley's Hall, the Matteson House, the Orient (St. James) Hotel, LaBerge's Hall, and many others. 350 of their tables have been put up, and are now in use in the city. Their trade extends from Canada to Mexico, and from the Alleghenies to the Pacific. Large rooms with their tables in every principal city in the West.

During an afternoon moment of relaxation, Moses Bensinger gets some liquid refreshment from Brunswick Vice-President A. F. Troescher.

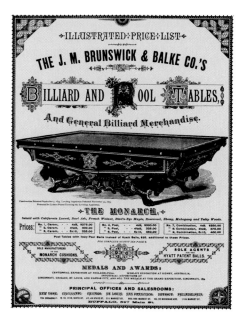

"EMANUEL BRUNSWICK & CO.'s BILLIARD-TABLE MAN-UFACTORY—47 and 49 State Street—was established in 1853; capital investment, $100,000; number of employees, 65; weekly payroll, $1,200; annual production, 450 tables, valued at $175,000. Mr. Brunswick is the oldest manufacturer in this line in the West . . . Messrs. Emanuel Brunswick & Co. have the finest billiard hall on this continent, on Washington Street, opposite the courthouse."

What is one to make of this?

The pages of Chicago city directories from the 1870s, though far from reliable or complete, present a dizzying number of Brunswick-operated businesses, at various locations. It makes for a strange puzzle, the solution to which has been buried by time. Whatever the nature of the relationships, Brunswick and his half-brothers eventually drifted apart. Emanuel, Joseph, and Hyman ran billiard parlors in such distant cities as San Francisco before eventually fading from the business. Solomon stayed in Cincinnati, where he devoted his time writing light verse for local newspapers.

In 1879, H. M. Collender, following the death of his father-in-law, Michael Phelan, joined forces with Brunswick and Balke. When the company was renamed the Brunswick-Balke-Collender Company in 1884, the capital stock was increased to $1.5 million. Shareholders' meetings began to be held regularly, and a board of directors was formed. Not only was the company the largest billiard equipment operation in the world, but it was larger than all competitors combined.

Moses Bensinger played a large role in the daily operations of the company, and as he concentrated on expanding the company to

THE PAREPA.

EXTREMELY DESIRABLE FOR ROOMS TOO SMALL FOR BILLIARD TABLES.
Size, 4x9 feet, with Eleven 2-inch Balls, Six Cues, Rack, Triangle, Black-Board, Small Balls, Bottle, and Ball Rack.
WOOD BED, PRICE, COMPLETE, $160 00.

VIRGINIUS.

AN EXTREMELY POPULAR GAME, AND THE LATEST IMPROVEMENT IN ELEVEN-BALL POOL TABLES.
Size, 4½x9 feet, with Eleven 2-inch Balls, Twelve Cues, One Cue Rack, Triangle, Small Balls, Bottle, and Ball Rack.
Slate Bed, Price, Complete, $175 00.   Wood Bed, Price, Complete, $150 00.

JENNY LIND.

WOOD BED, PRICE, COMPLETE, $140 00.
With Nine 2-inch Balls, Six Cues, Cue Rack, Black-Board, Rack, etc.
A very popular improvement on the Pigeon Hole, being a combination of that game with Bagatelle.

BAGATELLE.

PRICE, COMPLETE, $90 00.

THE ECLIPSE. 5

Our Billiard Lamps.—In towns where gas cannot be procured, or where it is too dear or too poor, our Monitor Eclipse Billiard Lamps render its absence a gain. Our Reflectors leave no shadow under the cushion, and the light is soft and pleasant. **PRICE, $8 00.**

PIGEON HOLE.

WOOD BED, PRICE, COMPLETE, $115 00.
With Nine 2-inch Balls, Six Cues, and Cue Rack.
This extremely attractive game is again rapidly growing into public favor.

THE MONITOR LAMP.

PRICE, COMPLETE, $8 00.

TEN PINS AND BALLS.

Good Balls and Pins are as necessary as a good alley to a good game, and we pay our greatest attention to the best material and finest, truest turning and workmanship. No sap surfaces or unseasoned material used. We have but one quality—the very best. Send for Monthly Price List.

The Brunswick catalogue was a feast of various products, among them some interesting and innovative variations on the game of billiards.

Though billiards was generally considered a man's game, one might still encounter a few accomplished woman players.

other cities, most notably Chicago, Brunswick remained in Cincinnati. The strain of business was apparent. Looking at rare pictures of him, one sees an imposing figure with sharp features and piercing eyes. He wore a beard in the style of the times and it made him appear as hard-edged and bone-tired as a Civil War general at the end of a bloody battle. But he continued to work long hours and became increasingly involved with local politics.

His interest had been kindled in 1870, when an admirer put his name into nomination on the Democratic ticket in his predominantly Republican ward. He lost that race by a surprisingly slender 48-vote margin. The next year, he was elected a Democratic state representative. He was an active legislator, introducing several important bills. One was an amendment to liquor laws whereby damages could be collected from "publicans, innkeepers and others, for assumed injury to the relatives or friends of inebriates." This law was an early version of the current Dram Shop Act. Another of his bills called for prohibition of the practice of pharmacy by anyone who hadn't passed an examination.

Still, he was at his factory every day, and it was there, on the hot afternoon of July 23, 1886, Brunswick suffered a heart attack while examining some billiard tables about to be shipped to Chicago. He was carried back to his home on Grandview Avenue and put to bed. Two days later, he was dead.

H. M. Collender took over as president of the firm. He was the logical choice. But he was an old man and quickly the jockeying for position under him grew intense. For four years, Collender did little more than keep track of the company's balance sheets and accept the growing number of medals and awards it was winning at international exhibitions for the quality of its tables, racks, cue sticks, and balls. He barely noticed the infighting that surrounded him, most loudly the battle between Bensinger and Leo Schmidt.

When Collender died in 1890, Julius Balke bowed to his own age and ill health and all but giftwrapped the presidency for the 51-year-old Bensinger. Schmidt was outraged and demanded out. Bensinger accommodated him, paying $300,000 for Schmidt's share of the firm.

Bensinger worked hard. And played hard, as noted in a frayed newsclipping: "An exciting race is scheduled to take place on the half-mile track at Crown Point, Indiana. It will be the old circus feat of man against horse, except that the race is to be modernized and the man mounted on a bicycle. Moses Bensinger will be the cyclist and the horse will be one of Will J. Davis' best trotters . . ."

Time has buried the race's outcome, but news of the event itself is a good example of Bensinger's character. This was a man who enjoyed challenges and risks. And was irresistibly drawn to products that would expand the company.

He reasoned that if tavern owners were in the market for a billiard table, they might also be interested in a bar. The company's woodworkers were designing

elaborate billiard tables, and it followed that their creativity would find a natural extension in making bars.

Though the prospering billiard business allowed for few idle moments at the company's factories, Bensinger began to fill them with the design of bars. The workers responded, fashioning structures at once magical and imposing—stunning meldings of rich woods, flawless mirrors, and stained glass into elegant pieces of furniture.

Originally the bars were built on special order, but demand grew so great that the company was soon selling as many front and back bars as it could make. As waves of immigrants began their steady flow

H. M. Collender, who served as Brunswick's president from 1886 to 1890, was busy gathering awards that the company's products, such as the back bar below, were winning at international exhibitions.

into this country, urban populations swelled and with them the number of taverns. Many of these were plain, seedy places where a man might get a glass of beer for a nickel. Some taverns, seeking to elevate themselves from their shabby brethren, purchased a Brunswick bar. It was a sure sign of elegance and respectability—a touch of class.

Orders came from all major cities. The bars were produced at a factory in Dubuque, Iowa, whose location on the Mississippi allowed easy shipment to Canada and other markets. The orders that came from San Francisco had to make their way by ship around Cape Horn at the tip of South America.

During the 1890s, newspapers were devoting space to the coverage of collegiate and professional sporting events. Little emphasis, however, was placed on participatory sports. The majority of Americans remained spectators.

Admittedly, there was a lot to see. Ice hockey was introduced to the U.S. in 1881, the year of the country's first lawn tennis match. Football scoring was standardized in 1884. Basketball was invented in 1891, golf tournaments began in 1894, professional football in 1895.

Most of these, however, with the exception of golf and tennis for the well-to-do, were not accessible or easily mastered by the proletariat. Bowling, on the other hand, was a middle-class delight. And Bensinger began to notice that many of the company's clients had installed bowling lanes in their taverns, and that those lanes were generally in use.

The popularity of bowling had grown steadily, if slowly, since it was first introduced to colonial America. An ancient game—a version of bowling is thought to have been played in Egypt as early as 5200 B.C.—it was first played on wide outdoor fields. Almost immediately it was set upon by Puritans, who believed it promoted gambling and laziness. The game, then called nine-pin bowls, or skittles, was banned in most of the 13 colonies. Eventually, some enterprising Connecticut settlers simply added a pin and argued

The careful craftsmanship of Brunswick's woodworkers is evident in this finely detailed section of a back bar produced in 1891.

with the authorities that the new game, ten-pin bowling, fell outside the prohibitory local ordinance.

The sport found its way indoors when restaurateurs and tavern owners realized they could attract customers by offering the amusement. They built lanes wherever they could, in basements or any sliver of space available. The first recorded indoor bowling match was played at the Knickerbocker Alleys in New York City on New Year's Day, 1840. At the time, there were some 200 alleys in New York alone, prompting one British visitor to note that "of all species of [participant] sports, bowling was the national one in America."

Over the next decades, however, the number of lanes was far outstripped by demand, and the quality of surfaces and equipment was sorry at best. To remedy these matters, a group of 27 men, representing nine bowling clubs in New York, met in 1875. After lengthy discussions in the Germania Hall in the Bowery, three of the day's finest players were authorized to revise the rules of the

sport, draft new laws, and submit their actions to a larger committee called the National Bowling Association.

This organization was short-lived, but it managed to enact a few important rules: The center of the head pin was to measure 60 feet from the bowler's end of the alley, or the foul line; fallen pins were to be removed from the alley; and all balls rolled in the gutter were declared dead.

As late as 1890, the sport of bowling was so disorganized that balls and pins varied dramatically in size. Rules for the sport were so confused that the fanciful scene and sure strike portrayed below could actually have taken place.

Jake Schaefer was one of billiards' early stars. Here he shows one reason why he was nicknamed "The Wizard."

In the cities, bowling proved an increasingly popular form of recreation. Here is a rare photograph of one of the first and best dressed women's leagues in New York City.

These rules were not universally accepted. Into the 1890s, the sport remained badly disorganized. The length of homemade lanes, the size of the balls and pins, and score-keeping methods varied widely.

But in this seeming chaos, Bensinger saw great potential. By the time he took over as president of Brunswick in 1890, he had already begun to oversee the company's first steps into the bowling business. As orders for pins, lanes, and wooden balls increased, he refined and enlarged Brunswick's capabilities to make them, carefully and quietly building a dominant company for a field in which domination was not yet warranted. He wanted to be at the starting line long before anyone else realized there was a race.

His influence had already been profoundly felt on the pastime of billiards. An accomplished player, he was frustrated by the fact that in three-carom billiards (otherwise known as straight-rail billiards), a good player could gather the three balls into one corner of the table and keep them there almost indefinitely while scoring.

The invention of the balkline— a thin chalk line drawn diagonally across each corner—and an early rule that allowed only one or two points to be scored consecutively within each triangular area helped little. Such stars as Jake "The Wizard" Schaefer spent the 1880s boasting that they had devised a method by which they could nurse balls gently against the rail, keep them close together, and score without missing as long as they desired.

Something had to be done, Moses realized, as he watched audiences doze during matches. He refined and perfected the balkline game, making it a challenge for the best players.

Equally interested in three-cushion and pocket billiards, his innovations there were of a technical rather than regulatory nature. He was constantly experimenting and researching, seeking better ways to make tables and equipment. A number of important patents for rubber cushions were registered in his name.

At best an average bowler, Moses had an even greater impact on that sport. He became bowling's biggest booster, bombarding the nation's leading bowling proprietors with letters. His argument was persuasive. The growth of the sport was stunted by its lack of standardized rules and equipment; if the sport were to grow it needed organization.

It took Bensinger five years to gather a group of bowlers and proprietors in New York City's Beethoven Hall. It was to be an informal get-together to discuss bowling rules and regulations. But by midnight of September 9, 1895, after hours of debate and eloquent speeches by Bensinger, the group had organized the American Bowling Congress.

He didn't stop there. He became the principal lobbyist for a national championship. And he got it in 1901, when the first ABC tournament was held in Chicago. Forty-one teams competed in the five-man event. The prize money was a substantial $1,200. Not coincidentally, all of the equipment used during that match, and for all ABC tourneys over the next 40 years, was manufactured by Brunswick.

Until Moses Bensinger convinced bowlers and proprietors of the need for a national bowling championship, most contests were impromptu affairs such as this 1892 battle.

4 *20th Century Unlimited*

Optimistic about the company's future, Moses Bensinger's son, Benjamin, prepares for further expansion and growth

More than a decade after the Chicago Fire of 1871 devastated the city, young B.E. Bensinger, Sr., began his career with Brunswick, sweeping floors in the company's factory.

In Cincinnati today, there are few vestiges of the Brunswick name. In the dusty files of the city's libraries and historical societies, one is lucky to find more than the briefest mention of the man or the company he built.

John Brunswick rode Cincinnati's boom years for all they were worth. But it was a later boom, in a bigger boom town, that eventually drew the company away from the banks of the Ohio to the shores of Lake Michigan.

Brunswick noticed Chicago's potential in the late 1840s, and over the next decades the city played an increasingly important role in the operations of the company. As the 1860s closed with a rush, Chicago was rich, the dominant city in the West. Its population was almost 300,000, nearly triple that at the beginning of the decade. The business district spread south and west from the river—79 bustling blocks of stores, hotels, and wholesale houses.

Potter Palmer, grown rich in merchandising and Civil War cotton speculation, owned three-fourths of a mile along State Street and was converting it to a street of merchants. There he built his Palmer House hotel and a "marble palace" that he leased to merchants Marshall Field and Levi Leiter. And there, two blocks south of the river and a block

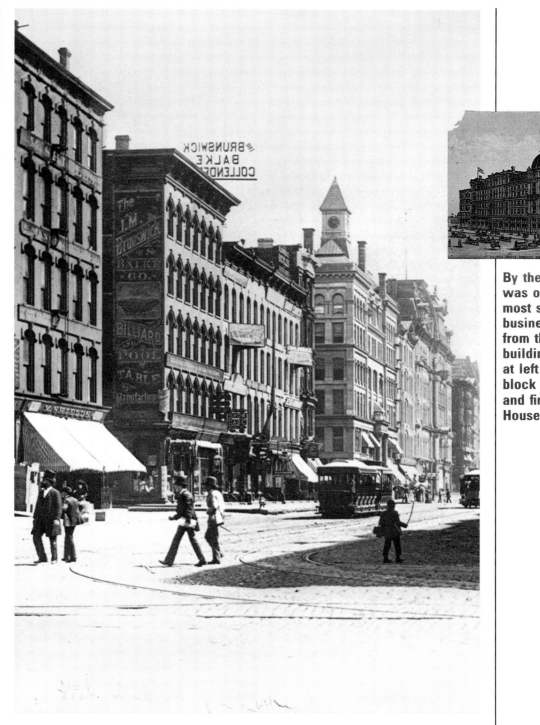

By the 1880s, Brunswick was one of Chicago's most successful businesses, operating from this five-story building on State Street, at left, just down the block from the famous, and fire-proof, Palmer House Hotel, above.

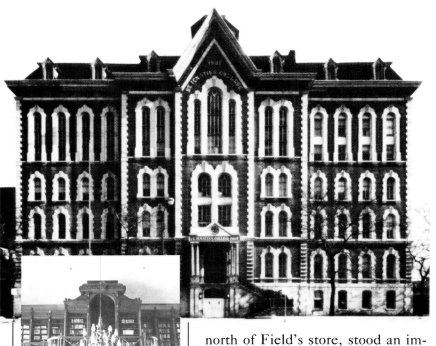

St. Ignatius College Prep was one of the few buildings to escape the Chicago Fire. It still stands today and houses this magnificent library built by Brunswick craftsmen in 1872.

north of Field's store, stood an imposing five-story building, with a huge sign on top: "J. M. Brunswick & Bros."

Even the events of Sunday evening, October 8, 1871, did little to set the company back. Only three days after the Chicago Fire finally burned itself out—with a property loss of $200 million, 250 dead, and 20,000 homes and 17,450 other buildings destroyed—the city was bouncing back. And so was Brunswick, open for business with new goods shipped from Cincinnati.

Only 20 years after the fire, the city was bigger than ever. By 1890, its population of 1,208,676 placed it second only to New York as the nation's major city. Sarah Bernhardt, on her first visit, performed for adoring theater crowds and paid the city compliments: "Chicago is the pulse of America.

I adore it." She also took note of the ambitious nature of its citizens: "It is a city in which men pass each other without even stopping, with knitted brows, with one thought in mind—the end to attain."

Chicago had an intoxicating effect on Moses Bensinger. He moved his family there in the 1880s, took offices in a State Street building and frequented the company's factories, one at Rush and Kinzie and the other at Huron and Sedgwick. The latter structure covered an entire city block; it contained a factory, warehouse, and lumber-drying plant built in stages from 1881 to 1883 at a cost of $168,165 and designed by the famous architect Louis Sullivan.

That is where Moses Bensinger put his son to work in 1885. Benjamin Bensinger was 17 years old then, a recent high school graduate. He began work as a clerk, filing order forms in the dark and musty warehouse. At nights he attended Bryant and Stratton Business College.

Shortly after John Brunswick's death in 1886, Moses formed a separate firm, the Bensinger Self-Adding Cash Register Company, and put Benjamin to work there as a salesman. He was taking no chances. There was no assurance that Moses would become President of Brunswick, as H. M. Collender had taken that position after John Brunswick's death.

But when Collender died in 1890 and Moses did take over as President he ended his association with the cash register firm and brought his son Benjamin back to Brunswick. Though Balke's son, Julius Jr., and John Brunswick's son, B. H., remained executives with the firm, neither would play important roles. And through the 1890's most corporate observers correctly assumed that Benjamin Bensinger was the most likely heir to the company.

Indeed, through his steady and determined climb up the corporate ladder, Benjamin was obviously being groomed to one day take the reins from his father. By 1896, the year he married Chicagoan Rose Frank, Benjamin was a manager in the company's Chicago offices, making the lordly sum of $200 a month, a salary higher than all but a couple of crack salesmen.

"My father was not happy making any except the finest quality goods," Benjamin once told a reporter. "We were a shirt-sleeve organization. Our doors were wide open, physically and mentally—as nearly as we could keep them that way—to any one with a case to state. I remember the great pains my father took to see that we were open-minded. He was personally acquainted with every employee in the business, and it was a fairly big business even then."

Horse drawn wagons delivered goods from the impressive Brunswick factory. Covering an entire city block north of the Chicago River, the building was designed by famous architect Louis Sullivan and completed in 1883.

Muskegon, Michigan, was a quiet town when Benjamin Bensinger decided to build a new factory there in 1906. An original 100,000-square-foot structure, as seen below in the 1920s, would eventually grow into a million-square-foot manufacturing plant.

At the time he assumed the company's presidency following his father's death on October 15, 1904, 36-year-old Benjamin headed a prosperous firm, with sales offices in a half-dozen American cities and in Canada and Mexico; there were manufacturing plants in Chicago, Cincinnati, Dubuque and New York. Because he anticipated great growth in the years ahead, Benjamin immediately began planning for the building of a major new manufacturing facility. As soon as news spread that the aggressive company was looking for a new home, Benjamin was deluged with attractive offers from cities throughout the Midwest.

Grand Rapids, Michigan, was especially persistent and made a persuasive pitch. And then, into Benjamin's office walked Charles Hackley and Thomas Hume, two convincing boosters of Muskegon, Michigan. They came prepared.

Having thoroughly researched the company and its needs, they sat down and talked for 30 minutes without interruption. Rattling off a mind-boggling series of facts and figures, they came on like a couple trying to marry off their homely daughter.

In a sense they were. Muskegon at the time was a tough sell. It was a homely town, desperately in need of a prosperous mate. It was little more than an overgrown village of less than 25,000 people. Its streets were paved with sawdust and cedar, its buildings and businesses shabby remnants of the days when the city had been a lumber boom-town known as "Sawdust City."

But, sitting 160 miles across Lake Michigan from Chicago, Muskegon would make a perfect stopping-off point for company-owned boats that carried cut maple from the company's lumber mill in Big Bay, Michigan, on Lake Huron; wood which, in turn, came from the 1,000 acres of timberland the

company owned near Lake Superior. Added to the desirability of its location was an ample work force.

Benjamin found the city most suitable, and on October 15, 1906, the company formally opened its 100,000-square-foot plant in Muskegon. One hundred newly hired employees and various local dignitaries gathered for the ribbon cutting ceremony. In charge of the operation was 29-year-old Fred Loewe, formerly an assistant to John Shank, production superintendent of all Brunswick plants.

Loewe was pleased with his new position, though he later remarked that when he and his family first arrived by train they had found Muskegon so unattractive "that we did all we could not to get back on the train." It was hard for him to imagine much excitement in this comparative backwater. He could not know that for the next 60-some years Muskegon would be the home of the company's most important plant.

Loewe looked around the opening day crowd until he spotted George Becker, supervisor of the billiard table assembly department, and J. O. Matteson, who headed the ball and chalk departments. They traded grin-and-bear-it shrugs.

The Light That Never Fails. As far as advertising slogans go, it is not particularly catchy. When you consider that it concerns an item that has nothing whatsoever to do with light, the phrase seems not only of dubious value but suspect effectiveness. But Benjamin Bensinger liked it.

"Let's go with it," he said in 1906, and his salesmen went out to sell a revolutionary rubber bowling ball dubbed the Mineralite. It was the invention of Michael J. "Dad" Whalen, a man whose zeal for inventions perfectly matched Bensinger's taste for new products.

Ships loaded with cut maple from Brunswick's lumber mill were frequent visitors to Muskegon's docks.

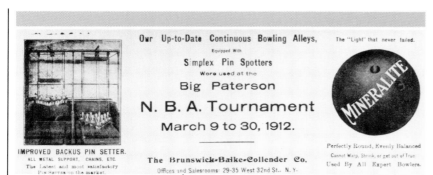

Our Up-to-Date Continuous Bowling Alleys,
Equipped With
Simplex Pin Spotters
Were used at the
Big Paterson
N. B. A. Tournament
March 9 to 30, 1912.

The "Light" that never failed.

MINERALITE

IMPROVED BACKUS PIN SETTER.
ALL METAL SUPPORT, CHAINS, ETC.
The Latest and most satisfactory
Pin Setter on the market.

The Brunswick-Balke-Collender Co.
Offices and Salesrooms: 29-35 West 32nd St., N. Y.

Perfectly Round, Evenly Balanced
Cannot Warp, Shrink, or get out of True.
Used By All Expert Bowlers.

The Mineralite vied for attention in this announcement with a less successful innovation, the forgotten Backus Pin Setter.

Though the American Hard Rubber Company of New York actually beat Brunswick's Mineralite to market by a few months, when the company unveiled its "Indestructible Hard Rubber Ball," the Mineralite proved far superior and quickly took the lion's share of the market, boosting bowling's popularity. It was vermillion in color and retailed for $20. That was a lot of money at the time, but the ball was guaranteed to hold its shape for three years, was chip-proof, and provided a consistency that made the old *lignum vitae* balls obsolete. It was also the first major success of the "rubber men."

Since the 1850s, Brunswick had been studying rubber and its uses, employing scientists to conduct experiments with the elastic substance. These generally eccentric fellows came to be known collectively as the "rubber men," and though they made minor improvements on billiard cushion patents, their work was relatively insignificant.

Whalen changed all that. While overseeing the production of the Mineralite at the company's Muskegon plant, he continued to experiment. Bensinger adored him. Giddy over the immediate success of the Mineralite ball, he became intrigued with rubber and its potential uses. He gave Whalen a free hand, often sending him letters full of ideas.

One night in 1912, after dinner at his Chicago home, Benjamin Bensinger sat brooding over an editorial he was reading. He crumpled the paper and threw it across the room. He was frustrated. At a time of unprecedented growth and expansion, the clouds of moral outrage again shadowed one of Brunswick's principal products and he didn't like it.

Billiards, bowling, and bars had a long history of conflict with America's moral arbiters. The two sports had each been able, thanks in large part to Brunswick's constant public relations efforts and its unassailable quality in materials and workmanship, to flourish in spite of repeated outcries against them. But bars—they were a different story. Benjamin sensed, in the vitriolic editorials he was reading, that the latest attacks against the evils of drinking were more serious than those of the past.

The cry for the banning of the sale, manufacture, and transportation of alcohol had begun in the early 1800s, intensifying during the reform movement of the 1830s and 1840s. In 1846, Maine passed the first state prohibition law. By 1855, 12 more states had followed suit. But support for the cause waned during the Civil War. The Prohibition Party, founded in 1869 in Chicago, was unable to compete politically against the established parties. The Women's Christian Temperance Union, founded in 1874 in the Chicago suburb of Evanston, was the first important national prohibition group, but it was limited by the political weakness of women.

The movement gained new momentum with the 1906 formation of the Anti-Saloon League, a group of prohibitionist preachers, teachers, and businessmen. Its growth was rapid, its influence national, and its political action intelligently managed. It was an

American ingenuity on the move: the revolutionary Mineralite bowling ball embarking on a world tour in 1914.

"THE POOR MAN'S CLUB."
THE MOST EXPENSIVE IN THE WORLD TO BELONG TO

A CLUB MEMBER IN GOOD STANDING
"PAYING HIS DUES"

unpleasant movement, tinged with bigotry and fueled by antipathy to the growth of cities, the presumed scene of most drinking.

As the attacks intensified, Brunswick launched a campaign to persuade voters that prohibition was a bad idea. It wasn't working. Some papers, such as the *Montreal Observer,* lambasted the company:

"The Brunswick-Balke-Collender Co., of Toronto, whiskey concern, has issued an enormous poster for the guidance of newspapers and voters. According to this poster, which has been sent to nearly all the papers in Canada, it is wrong for voters to vote for prohibition. Whiskey makes trade and gives people work and for this rea- son, asserts the poster, the voters should see to it that their candidate does not favor prohibition. The temperance sentiment is growing so strong that the whiskey makers have become thoroughly alarmed and are using every possible means for the influencing of the public against the destruction of their business . . . Rather does it influence all good citizens to so vote as to compel your directors, even against their own inclinations, to earn a living by some means not harmful to the body politic."

That sort of stinging response was not exclusive to Canada,

where prohibition laws were finally adopted in 1915. A growing number of American newspapers expressed similar sentiments, though rarely in such terms.

Brunswick continued to fill orders for its bars and a number of related accessories and fixtures such as beer glass shelves, bottle cases, railings, gates, food and beverage coolers, lunch counters, and window screens. But Benjamin Bensinger grew pessimistic and in preparation for what he felt was the inevitable, he began cutting back on production of the lavish and expensive bars.

Over three icy days in 1912, workmen began loading on trains Brunswick's considerable stock of fixtures in Kansas City. Sales had almost ceased there because of the prohibition movement, and the goods were to be moved to Chicago, where sales remained fairly strong.

An enterprising reporter from the *Kansas City Star,* a staunch advocate of prohibition, chanced to see the fixtures and bars being loaded for their trip north. He spent days digging up what facts he could. His story, claiming that Brunswick was running scared, caused considerable panic. Most of the country's tavern owners wanted to believe that prohibition would never arrive, and they looked to Brunswick as the most

knowledgeable source, and reliable barometer, on the issue. The story out of Kansas City caught everyone off guard and though prohibition was still nine years off, for all practical purposes Brunswick was out of the bar business.

"We eventually disposed of all our stock without loss, but it would have been the plainest folly to go on manufacturing more in that line," Bensinger later recalled. "We discontinued manufacturing bar fixtures at once and immediately looked around for some other business. . . ."

The Brunswick catalogue contained such practical items as this lavish beer cooler and such playful items as these decorative mirrors.

Convex Mirrors.
REVOLVING.

Very amusing, and an attractive piece of saloon furniture.
The mirror revolves on pivot attached to the wall.

PRICES WITH FRAME.

18 x 24, - - - - $10.05
18 x 32, - - - - 16.30

5

A Taste for Innovation

As billiards boom, Brunswick enters the prosperous but precarious automobile and music businesses

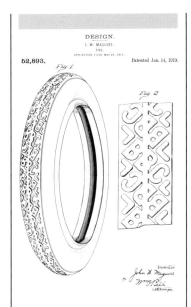

It was the tremendous popularity of billiards that enabled Benjamin Bensinger to enter such new fields as the manufacture of automobile tires which were emblazoned with the company's initials.

After nearly 70 years of unbridled success, Brunswick faced its first crisis when the prohibition movement knocked out the bar and bar fixture business. With it went $4 million in sales, nearly one-fourth of the company's annual revenue.

Some executives might have headed for the nearest tavern or highest window ledge. Benjamin Bensinger had a different idea—to quickly find a new business which might best utilize the company's existing manufacturing facilities.

The company was by no means in a dire situation. It was making not only billiard tables, but balls and cues and other equipment; bowling balls and equipment; a complete line of church furniture, and the interior wood trim for churches, banks and commercial buildings. And the irrepressible Whalen was keeping things percolating in Muskegon. Benjamin sent Whalen notes filled with his observations on Chicago streets. Just as his grandfather had noticed the potential of the carriage trade on the streets of New York, so Benjamin had begun to think highly of the automobile business.

Cars careened all over Chicago streets. The city's first automobile club was formed in 1906, and by 1909 the Sears, Roebuck and Company mail-order catalogue was

Helping to keep the jazz in the Jazz Age, Brunswick became a leading music maker during the 1920s.

trumpeting its "Motor Buggy . . . a practical car for use every day in the year over rural and city roads." The price: $395.

Whalen responded. A group of engineers under his charge made the first Brunswick tire in 1912. Actual production, however, did not begin for four more years since Whalen was onto something in which he saw greater potential than tires. That something was toilet seats.

In 1912, the company introduced its Whale-Bone-Ite, the first rubber toilet seat. It was a sensation.For a country accustomed to the rigors of wooden toilet seats, the Whale-Bone-Ite was greeted with almost tearful gratitude. A major purchaser was the Pullman Company, the nation's largest manufacturer of railroad passenger cars. Hotels unabashedly advertised, among their classiest amenities, "the comfort of the new toilet seats." Hospitals, offices, schools, and government

buildings were eager customers. As Americans breathed a collective sigh of relief, production of the seats quickly reached a peak of 120,000 a year.

The tire business could wait. Bensinger felt no urgency to enter that market. At first, it seemed too modest. In 1914, there were only 1.3 million cars on America's dusty roads. Instead, he looked for other ways to use the men and machines idled by the cessation of the bar furnishings business. He considered many, from an expansion of the company's furniture line to building automobile bodies.

It was an employee in the company's Chicago factory who offered the first solution: piano cases. It seemed perfect. The cases called for the highest skill in the woodworker's craft, and there was no American company more renowned for its art with wood. The cases could be made in the company's factories without much adjustment. They could be sold in large

Invented by J. "Dad" Whalen and the "rubber men" in Muskegon, the Whale-Bone-Ite was America's first rubber toilet seat.

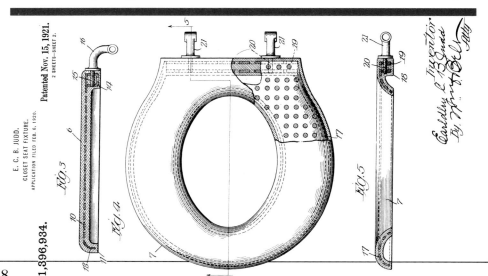

quantities to piano manufacturers, which would mean only a slight reorganization of the company's sales force.

The plan was put into action. Aided by the company's record for quality production, orders quickly reached sufficient number to keep nearly all of the under-employed woodworking facilities busy. Unfortunately, two years later, the piano business slumped badly and the company was back at square one. Bensinger, who put great faith in his employees and in plain thinking, instructed his sales force to look through newspapers and determine from advertisements what might be a fertile growth industry for the company. It was a deceptively simple strategy.

"Look through the newspapers, boys," Bensinger said. "And find me something we can make."

That something was phonograph cabinets. "We wrote a letter one morning to all the principal phonograph manufacturers asking if they would be interested in bids on phonograph cases," Bensinger recalled, as refreshingly matter-of-fact as if discussing a trip to the barbershop. "They knew of our work in the old lines and more particularly of our work in piano cases during the last years. Out of that letter and some brief negotiations came an order for $1 million worth of phonograph cases."

The company's principal client for the cases was the Edison Phonograph Company. And its timing was perfect, for a dance mania swept the land. Under the heading "New Reflections on the Dancing Mania," a magazine called *Current Opinion* declared in childlike wonder: "People who have not danced before in 20 years have been dancing, during the past summer, afternoons as well as evenings. Up-to-date restaurants provide a dancing floor so that patrons may lose no time while the waiters are changing the plates. Cabaret artists

Brunswick's craftsmen used their woodworking skills to create phonograph cabinets both handsome and functional.

are disappearing except as interludes while people recover their breaths for the following number. One wishes either to dance or to watch and to criticize those who dance." Record sales soared as tangos, one-steps, hesitation waltzes, and turkey trots came flowing off the presses.

Though the demand for phonographs was exceptional, Bensinger was not particularly pleased. Instead of patting himself on the back, he asked himself how he could make the best of a good situation. Finally it hit him: Brunswick should begin making and selling its own phonographs.

That idea made the company's executives nervous.

"Are you sure?" one asked him. "Don't you think it's a bit foolhardy to give up what's become a very lucrative line for . . . for what? Do we know how to make phonographs?"

"Someone in this company must know how to make one of those things," Bensinger said with typical confidence. "You've seen them. How hard could they be to make?"

He pushed ahead, motivated by what he felt an affront to the traditions of the company. "We were making cabinets in our own best style, and they were sold under a trade name not our own," he explained. "Cabinets were the most difficult part of the phonograph to manufacture, and the salesmanship of machines centered most heavily on aesthetics. It was the style and quality of the cabinets, rather than their tonal quality, that was most important to the first generation of phonograph buyers. We were building good will, so far as this line was concerned, only with a few manufacturers and not the general public. This was a far different situation than with our plan with billiard tables, bar fixtures, and the rest."

Furthermore, sales initiative in the line was largely in the hands of others. Whatever fine ideas Brunswick had for promoting the sales of phonographs were cannibalized by its customers, and not always to the best effect. These

The first Brunswick record was pressed in 1922, and it was followed by a steady stream of discs featuring many of the biggest stars and sweetest voices of the day.

were not the rules by which Brunswick liked to play. This was a company very uncomfortable as middleman.

Bensinger started to search through the company for someone who might make a prototype of the Brunswick phonograph. He visited the company's various factories. At the large plant in Muskegon he came across two fellows who expressed interest in the project.

"Have you ever made one?" Bensinger asked.

"How hard could it be?" they answered.

Benjamin Bensinger admired that sort of confidence. He had an insatiable appetite for new businesses and new products, and the sort of people who could produce them. He was always eager, in the days before research and development teams, to put free-lance inventors on his payroll.

"Here's $50," Bensinger told the two eager phonograph makers. "Go into town and buy whatever you need and build a couple of different models. When you're finished, send them to me in Chicago."

He returned to the company's offices in Chicago and waited. By April 3, 1916, the machines were ready. Surrounded by the members of the board of directors, Bensinger slowly rose from his chair and began to read: "There is the likelihood that the present contract with the Edison Phonograph Company will not be

Keeping the books was still a fairly simple matter as a distinguished-looking Benjamin Bensinger led the company through tremendous growth during the 1920s.

renewed . . . It was, after considerable discussion, decided to take up the manufacture of complete phonographs in two different styles."

At that moment, a pair of secretaries walked in toting the two experimental machines. They placed them at either end of the long table. Board members rose and surrounded the machines as if exploring toys on Christmas morning. A few minutes later, the phonographs were turned on and music poured through the room.

"I may have been prejudiced," Bensinger said. "But the machines didn't seem to work so bad."

On April 20, it became official: "This is an advance notice of our intention to put a high-grade

The cover of Brunswick's 1923–24 catalogue was adorned by elephants, while the inside contained page after page of equally impressive creations, such as the table below.

phonograph on the market," read a press release. "Samples together with advertising matter will be ready inside of sixty days. We expect to have the department in full swing considerably on the hitherto side of the holidays . . ."

"Our best quality machine, which will compare favorably with any high-grade machine on the market sold at $250, will list at about $150. This will be the same quality of cabinets that we are now producing for other makes of $250 machines. The tone arm and sound box will be gold plated. The motor will be Swiss-American, and best of all it will be provided with both Emerald or Black Diamond points, and regulation needles, so that it will play any of the four styles of records on the market . . ."

It was a good year, 1916, full of activity. As well as its new line of phonographs, Whalen and his "rubber men" were ready to put Brunswick automobile tires on America's roads. There was no way of predicting the future

of these new endeavors. But bolstered by the burgeoning popularity of billiards, Bensinger could afford to enter these precarious new fields.

The envelope contained a gold embossed brochure announcing the opening of Will Graney's billiard parlor in San Francisco. Benjamin Bensinger studied the photographs of the room's 42 tables. They were Brunswick tables, the finest ever made—sturdy and imposing, with intricate ivory inlays and mesh leather pockets festooned with gold tassels. Above them hung row after row of lights, and between them sat red leather club chairs, tables, and large, shimmering brass cuspidors. A smile lit Benjamin's face.

Make no mistake about his priorities. As voracious as he was for new products, Benjamin was keenly aware that billiards provided the financial foundation and solid reputation that enabled him

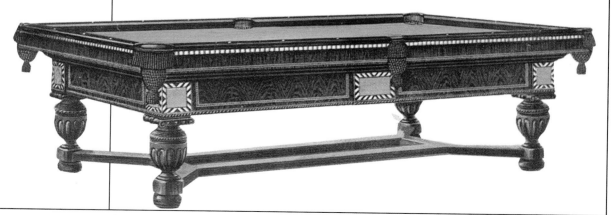

during the 1910s and 1920s to venture into other businesses.

Billiards was his considerable bankroll. It is difficult today to comprehend how popular billiards was during the early decades of this century, especially when one realizes that until 1906, the game had a serious image problem.

It took a boy to change America's mind. Willie Hoppe was an ingenuous 18-year-old from Cornwall Landing, Long Island, when he sailed to Paris for a billiard match against Maurice Vignaux, then considered the greatest player in the world.

On the night of January 15, 1906, Hoppe stood across the table from Vignaux. They were playing to 500 points and the old master led, 266 to 228.

"The few Americans in the crowd didn't look too happy," Hoppe recalled. "The positions of the balls were marked with a pencil. The referee handed the ball to my father, who nursed it in his pocket throughout intermission to keep it warm. When we resumed, I kept close enough until I finally ran 93. That put me solidly in front at 417 to 295. I got the necessary 83 in two innings, one being a string of 75. When I went to bed that night I clutched a gold watch and chain and nearly $1,000 in cash, presents from my backers."

The next day, American newspapers headlined the victory of the "Boy Wonder." Hoppe returned to America a national hero. In Hoppe, America found the sort of virtuous young man any Bible belt mother could adore—a drab, non-smoking teetotaler who belied every commonly held image of the pool room denizen. The image of billiards began to change as Hoppe travelled throughout the country, giving exhibition matches in front of huge crowds. For him, it was work. For America, it was the beginning of a golden age in sports. In Detroit, fans filled the baseball park to witness the feats of a surly, talented rookie named Cobb. And they would soon be cheering the exploits of an ill-fated Indian athlete named Thorpe, a portly fellow named Ruth, a graceful tennis player named Tilden . . . and so many others. In less than a decade, American games were transformed from mildly amusing diversions into national spectacles.

Billiards was as popular as any sport. By the 1920s, there were more than 42,000 poolrooms in the United States, 4,000 in New York. In other cities, lavish parlors became minor urban landmarks and tourist attractions. One could play on the 42 tables at Ling and Allen in Kansas City, Sol Allinger's 37 tables, or the 70 tables at Hudson Recreation Center in Philadelphia. They could rack them up at Pope Sibley's 30 tables in Seattle or the 88 tables in the W. P. Mussey poolroom in Chicago's Loop. And how about the 142 tables in Detroit's Recreation?

After returning from his triumphant win over billiard master Maurice Vignaux in Paris, the straight-laced Willie Hoppe toured America and gave a jolt to billiards' popularity.

Jim Thorpe, shown in his football outfit, and Ty Cobb were among the talented athletes who turned America's sports from mere games into national spectacles.

At the Graney in San Francisco, one could mingle with socialites and hustlers in the Billiard Academy, a backroom playing area with a 400-seat spectator gallery—the nation's first, last, and only billiard casino.

Along with these great halls came a generation of famous players. They were household names—Hoppe and three-cushion stars like Augie Kiekhefer, Charles Peterson, Johnny Layton, and Bob Cannefax; pocket-billiard players like Alfredo DeOro, Emmett Blankenship, Frank Taberski, and Erwin Rudolphe.

The best and the brightest was Ralph Greenleaf. Unlike Hoppe, Greenleaf was a born showman, a fast-living and supremely talented player, a virtual model of Jazz Age attributes. He won his first title in 1919, held it for six years, and

continued to win it on and off, until capturing his fourteenth crown in 1937.

Between tournaments he and his wife, the equally exuberant Princess Nai Tai Tai, toured the Orpheum vaudeville circuit, making as much as $2,000 a week putting on trick shot exhibitions on a table over which hung huge mirrors that gave the audience a view of the entire playing surface.

By the end of the 1910s, Brunswick was selling tables as fast as they could be produced at its eight factories in the East and Midwest. Chicago had become the company's official executive headquarters in 1908, when it dissolved its Ohio Corporation and incorporated in the state of Delaware. Its sales headquarters were in Muskegon, from where it ran a dealer network of 27 U.S. offices,

five in Canada, plus overseas showrooms in London, Paris, Buenos Aires, Honolulu and Mexico City. Brunswick owned more than a thousand acres of hardwood timberland near Lake Superior, including a saw mill, lumber camp, general store, boarding houses, repair shops, a small railroad and steamboats to carry the lumber from its Big Bay landing to Muskegon.

The company owned its own slate quarries in Vermont and Pennsylvania. It was the world's largest user of hardwood. Its annual output of cues alone was more than 400,000, and it had enough reserve maple in its drying kilns (which were also the world's largest) to make an additional 600,000.

Any self-respecting billiard parlor proprietor filled his parlor with Brunswick tables, and the company was continually expanding its line to meet the various needs of its customers. The choice was wide. From the more than 15 models offered, one could choose the medium-priced Madison (1,950 pounds and finished in mahogany with white holly inlay, black border, and eggshell gloss), the Regal, the Regina, or the Sterling. And there was the majestic, top-of-the-line Arcade, a six-legged wonder of 2,760 pounds.

Brunswick's tables and equipment were the latest word in playing appointments. And its po-

sition of leadership in the business enabled it to direct official tournament billiards in the United States from the 1880s until the 1970s. For a time, it even owned copyrights on the official rule and record book.

Brunswick's determined effort to make billiards respectable for the middle class is dramatized by this persuasive advertisement from the Saturday Evening Post.

The young and stylish Duke Ellington was among the brightest stars on the Brunswick label.

It was Al Jolson, in his most famous pose, who made company cash registers ring with his best-selling "Sonny Boy."

The biggest-selling record of late 1919 was a catchy little song called "Alice Blue Gown." It was being played on many of the more than 2 million phonographs turned out that year by 200 American manufacturers. Four years earlier, there had been only 18 phonograph makers. But as the 1920s began, customers were jamming into stores, falling over themselves to buy the latest models.

Brunswick's phonograph business, which had shown an $18,000 loss during its first year, 1916, turned a handsome $703,000 profit three years later. Workers at the Muskegon plant could be heard whistling as production reached 750 phonographs a day.

Muskegon was a hotbed of activity. By 1921, with 10.5 million autos in the country, Brunswick was making more than 2,000 tires a day in Muskegon. But the company was but one of more than two dozen fighting for a share of the market. It became increasingly difficult to keep pace with those companies that had concentrated technology and better focused marketing strategy. The company might have been able to slug it out for a while, but when the price of rubber nearly tripled in 1922, Bensinger was left with no choice but to reluctantly discontinue the tire operation.

It was a pleasant surprise, and an indication of the company's name in the marketplace, when B. F. Goodrich approached the company for the rights to produce a tire under the Brunswick name, which it did the following year, forming the Brunswick Tire Corporation.

This experience soured Benjamin Bensinger on the rubber business and compelled him to boldly take the company further

into the music business. Among the many reasons was that he did not enjoy listening to someone else's records spinning on Brunswick machines.

In order to make its own music, the company set up studios in New York. In January 1922, the first disc under the Brunswick label was pressed. An impressive collection of recording stars were soon signed to exclusive contracts—Duke Ellington, Benny Goodman, Cab Calloway, Montana Taylor, Red Nichols and his Five Pennies, and the wonderfully named Speckled Red and Cow Cow Davenport. The "Brunswick Hall of Fame" label signed such major classical performers as Richard Benelli, Mario Chamlee, Irene Pavlovska, and Leopold Godowsky.

This new industry proved extremely volatile and highly competitive. But Brunswick was a seasoned marketplace fighter. When the upstart radio industry threatened the phonograph business, the company responded quickly and began selling radios, forming an agreement in 1924 with the Radio Corporation of America to install RCA's popular Radiolas in Brunswick phonographs. RCA was at the forefront of a mushrooming industry. In Chicago in 1924, there were 30,000 receivers and a dozen radio stations.

And still more. In 1925, Brunswick collaborated with the General Electric Company to produce an all-electric phonograph. Called the

Panatrope, it came in various models (with or without radio) for $350 and up. It was a revolutionary item, the first electric phonograph on the market, and for it Brunswick and GE developed a new system of electrical recording.

Things could not have been more exciting, and the future could not have looked brighter. By 1928, Brunswick's sales topped $29 million. Emotions were running so carefree at corporate headquarters that when Al Jolson's 1929 Brunswick recording of "Sonny Boy" topped the pop music charts, the singer was made a member of the company's board of directors.

The ebullient Cab Calloway made beautiful music for Brunswick.

6 *Surviving the Storms*

The Depression rocks Brunswick, but Bob and Ted Bensinger preserve the company and enable it to respond to the War Effort

Taking over the company presidency in 1930, Bob Bensinger was determined to bring modern management methods to Brunswick and lead it boldly into its second century.

Robert Frank Bensinger, the eldest son of Benjamin Bensinger, was a handsome, successful, and generally happy young man as he sat down to breakfast at his home in the Chicago suburb of Glencoe one morning in the late 1920s. He read a story in the morning paper. It was an amazing story: Chicago teachers were being paid in scrip. This was the latest in a series of bad economic signs that peppered the morning papers.

In many ways Bob Bensinger felt beyond harm. The recent ripples in the American economy—the huge drop in housing starts, the inability of municipalities to meet their bills, the rising unemployment—did not seem likely to affect Glencoe. And Brunswick was thriving.

He could not have known that the disturbing stories in the papers were harbingers of the Great Depression. He had little experi-

They helped build airplanes and they helped keep things humming at Brunswick's plants. At the outset of World War II, women joined the workforce in great numbers.

Gatherings of the unemployed were frequent sights during the 1930s as hundreds of companies went belly up.

ence with trouble, economic or otherwise. Born on February 10, 1898, in Chicago, Bob was raised in considerable comfort, as was his younger brother Ted, born in 1905. Bob attended Lake Forest Academy in suburban Chicago, Phillips Exeter Academy in New Hampshire, and he had been headed for an Ivy League education when World War I interrupted. He enlisted in the Navy. Returning from sea in 1919, he went to work for Brunswick and his father.

"My father was a tough taskmaster," Bob recalled. "He was a wonderful man but didn't believe in spoiling his sons."

Bob's first job was in the Muskegon plant, sweeping floors. Later he drove horse wagons—fetching and loading lumber at the docks, toting it back to the factory, checking it, counting it. Near the end of his two year Michigan stay, he tried his hand at the family's oldest trade. Working alone, he spent a month building his own billiard table.

He was not unhappy when summoned back to Chicago for a position in the credit department. During the next few years, he worked in every department of the company, developing a facility for dealing with bowling and billiard customers, and learning to speak their hard-edged language. In 1922, he was elected to the Board of Directors and he became a Vice-President three years later.

In appearance he closely resembled his father, with dark hair, a firm jaw line, and deeply expressive eyes. And it was assumed that he would eventually take his father's place as the President of Brunswick. Thoughts of that future were often on his mind some mornings in 1929 as he pored carefully over the news in the morning papers, little aware of the storms the next few years would hold for himself and Brunswick.

Moving east, the 20th Century Limited carried Benjamin Bensinger and his son Bob to New York and a $10 million deal.

One night in 1930, The 20th Century Limited rode through darkness from Chicago to New York. Aboard the train were Benjamin Bensinger and his eldest son, Bob. They did not sleep. When they arrived at Grand Central Station their sleeping compartment was a shambles, spread with hundreds of pieces of paper. They gathered their work and headed for a meeting with Harry Warner, the president of Warner Brothers Pictures.

Warner Brothers was one company that seemed able to weather the Depression. Its revolutionary Vitaphone talkies, most notably "The Jazz Singer," were setting box office records across the country.

Early in 1930, Warner had approached Brunswick about acquiring its phonograph and recording businesses. Warner wasn't really interested in the machines themselves. Instead, he saw great advantages in owning a record line on which he could promote and sell Warner film stars.

Benjamin Bensinger, and no doubt Warner, too, knew that Brunswick was in a bad bargaining position. The company had gone public in 1924 and, like most companies at the time, it had begun paying huge dividends to shareholders instead of building a cash surplus. Once the Depression hit, the banks began clamoring for the $9 million Brunswick owed. "And my father hated to owe so much money," recalled Bob.

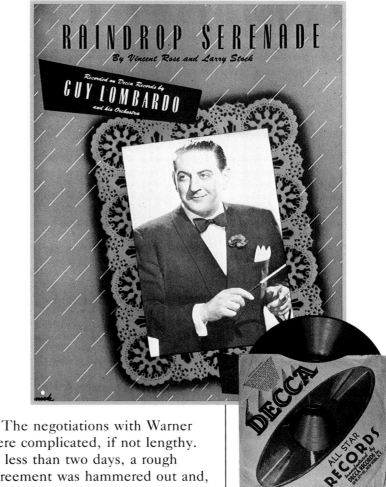

Eventually many of the biggest Brunswick stars, among them Guy Lombardo, left Warner Brothers for other recording companies such as the aggressive new Decca label.

The negotiations with Warner were complicated, if not lengthy. In less than two days, a rough agreement was hammered out and, on April 9, 1930, a 42-page contract was signed. "I think it was the smartest deal my father ever made," Bob said years afterward. "It helped save the company."

What proved a good deal for Brunswick provided nothing but headaches for Warner Brothers. Two years later, in 1932, record sales fell to six percent of what they had been during the late 1920s, and Warner Brothers turned the Brunswick catalogue and trademark over to the American

Record Company, a producer of bargain-priced 35 cent discs sold at Woolworth and similar chain stores. ARC continued to sell the more popular Brunswick performers on 75 cent records.

David and Jack Kapp, brothers who owned a small jazz record store in Chicago, changed that. Joining forces with a canny London stockbroker named E. R. Lewis, the Kapps formed Decca Records and persuaded most of the Brunswick "75 cent artists"

that they would sell more records, and lose no prestige, if they were on lower priced discs. Bing Crosby, the Dorsey Brothers, Guy Lombardo, the Mills Brothers and others joined the Decca label.

ARC was eventually purchased for $700,000, by William Paley, president of the Columbia Broadcasting System. Decca and the record industry flourished. Celebrating its fifth anniversary in 1938, Decca announced sales of 19 million records. Its "A-tisket, A-tasket" sold more than 300,000 copies, more than tripling the sales of former Brunswick board member Al Jolson and his "Sonny Boy." The value and reputation of the Brunswick label, however, was undeniable as its name continued to live on records into the 1950s.

The repeal of Prohibition in 1933 was the cause for many happy celebrations. It also prompted Brunswick to resume its bar and bar fixture business.

Warner Brothers paid roughly $10 million for the Brunswick Panatrope & Radio Corporation and, more importantly, "certain assets pertaining to the Musical Division." Using the money from the sale to pay off the company's bank loans, Benjamin Bensinger took the newly created position of Chairman of the Board and Bob took over as President. Through the dark days and uncertainty, Bob managed as best he could to keep the company alive.

"Things were very bad," Bob Bensinger said, recalling the Depression years. "We were forced to cut salaries three times in a period of two years. We tried everything not to eliminate people. We thought it better to cut salaries than let people go. But it was bad. We did eventually have to lay some people off. If we hadn't, we couldn't have survived. It hurt me so much, so very much."

Hundreds, even thousands, of companies did not survive the Depression. Chicago and its businesses were especially hard hit. By 1933, the number of people employed in the city was cut in half. Payrolls were down 75 percent. Foreclosures jumped five-fold, and more than 150 banks failed. Families evicted from their homes were living in the city's parks.

A godsend, of sorts, came in 1933 with the repeal of the 18th amendment and the company's guarded resumption of its bar fixture business. That industry had changed. No longer was there demand for expensive bars. Still, the company's tavern salesmen were greeted by tavern owners with the sort of affection usually reserved for fraternity brothers at a college reunion. The salesmen did not come empty handed. They offered a revolutionary table-top refrigerator called the "Blue Flash" and the response from institutional as well as home markets was enthusiastic.

Thus encouraged, the company began marketing a line of soda fountains in 1935. Though Brunswick had been making such items on a minor scale since the 1920s, the Depression had transformed the minor into major. The fountains were quickly followed by such items as the "Rubberceptor," a "leak-proof, safe, quiet, and sanitary" shower stall floor.

Brunswick's revolutionary Blue Flash—a table top refrigerator that was one of the company's most successful products during the 1930's.

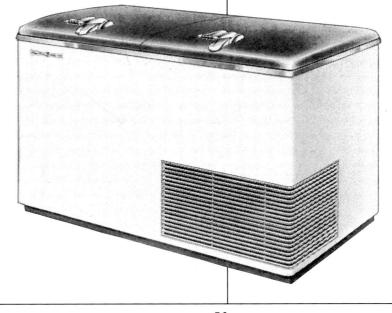

The success of these goods was not spectacular, especially when compared to the profits of some of the company's pre-Depression products. But it was steady. It gave Brunswick financial breathing room, supplementing the greatly decreased cash flow generated by the sale of bowling and billiard equipment.

Though the thousands of pool parlors around the country were experiencing a boom, thanks to the tens of thousands of idle workers who found the rooms fine places to spend their time, the sales of new tables were virtually non-existent.

By the time Benjamin Bensinger died, on November 27, 1935, he had sadly watched his company shrink to the size it had been, and assume the general appearance it had at the turn of the century.

Company sales had fallen to a low of $3.9 million in 1932 from $29.5 million in 1928, and there was trouble collecting debts. During the early 1930s, the company's losses averaged $1 million a year.

One Chicago morning in the summer of 1938, a young man walked nervously south along Chicago's Wabash Avenue. Above him, the sun filtered through the wooden planks of the elevated train. Joseph Stefan watched his reflection in the windows along the street. It was just six blocks from the Marshall Field store, where he worked in the legal department, to his destination. But it seemed to be taking forever. Stefan had an 11:30 a.m. appointment with Julius Hoffman, a Brunswick

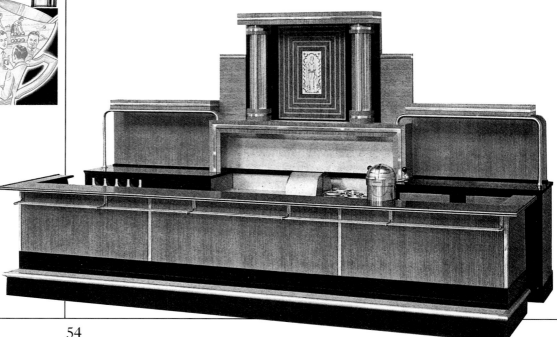

Vice President and General Counsel. Actually, the meeting was a job interview. He had heard from a former classmate at Northwestern University law school that Brunswick was actively recruiting "bright young men."

Finally, he stood in front of the company's 10-story building at 623 South Wabash. Stefan straightened his tie, buttoned his coat, took a deep breath and walked inside.

"I'll never forget it," he remembered years later. "It was . . . well, quite unbelievable. You must understand that I had been working at the Field building, and that it was a beautiful and very modern structure. The Brunswick place was something altogether different. The first thing I saw was a man in a cashier's cage, the old-fashioned sort, surrounded by wire. He was even wearing a green eyeshade. The elevators were open and rickety. Everything was so antiquated. Looking around that lobby for the first time I was tempted to turn around and run back to Field's. I felt like I'd stepped back in time."

The office of Julius Hoffman, who was later to gain fame as the federal judge presiding at the trial of a group known as the Chicago Seven, was on the fourth floor. Stefan's interview lasted more than an hour. Simpson E. Meyers, then head of the credit department, was also present.

"It was an intense session," Stefan said. "The company was eager to revitalize. It was seeking new

blood. The Depression had not been kind but the company was determined to fight back."

Leading the battle was Bob Bensinger, with the help of his younger brother, Ted. The brothers agreed that if Brunswick was to

The Studebaker Building on Chicago's Wabash Avenue became the Brunswick headquarters after a fire destroyed the company's previous home in 1913. Brunswick occupied the entire building until moving to more modern quarters in 1964.

be revived, it would have to undergo a major facelift, and so would the pastimes on which it depended. They ordered a management survey, the first in the company's history.

"It was an important move," said Bob. "We wanted a close look at weaknesses in individuals and

Remaining a leader in the recreation field, Brunswick filled orders for equipment from USO clubs and military centers, where troops got a chance for some relaxation.

departments. The report made a lot of recommendations. Some we followed, some not."

The effect was that of a general housecleaning. It led to the retirement of many executives and gave the company its introduction to modern management methods.

Brunswick's appearance in the summer of 1938 was deceiving. On the surface it had the shabby look of a battle-scarred survivor. But Stefan, and the many other "bright young men" visiting the offices at the time, were struck by the firm's energy and optimism. That is why, when Julius Hoffman stood up and said to Stefan, "We would like you to work for us," the young lawyer did not hesitate.

"Wonderful," he said.

"When can you start?" asked Hoffman.

"I've got to tell them at Field's and . . ."

"Well, the sooner the better," said Hoffman.

As the Depression eased and employment rose, poolroom attendance began to fall off for the first time in history. Initially, few at Brunswick noticed for there was a large, immediate demand for tables and equipment from a new source: USO clubs and military centers. World War II was on.

Brunswick was no stranger to defense production. During World War I, the company had supplied gun stocks and wooden wings for fighter planes. The company's first World War II government contract was for parachute bomb flares, used to illuminate areas during bombing raids. Other items followed: assault boats and aircraft fuselages, and floors and landing skids for Air Force gliders. B. F. Goodrich worked with Brunswick to supply self-sealing fuel cells for aircraft and floating mines. Brunsalloy, a lightweight but extremely strong metal alloy, was developed and used effectively as a substitute for aluminum in aircraft production.

From the plant in Muskegon poured these things and more: 60mm illuminating mortar shells, aircraft instrument panels, and aluminum litters. The plant easily handled the work, adapting smoothly from making the tools of play to fashioning the items of war; the place had grown, since 1906, into a one-million-square-foot operation.

Thanks to government contracts and the effects of its recent housecleaning, Brunswick was able to post sales of $20 million in 1942. Throughout the war, the company not only proved capable of making sophisticated products, thereby laying the foundation for today's Defense Division, but continued its dominance in the recreation field. By 1945, more than 13,000 billiard tables and 3,000 bowling lanes had been installed at military and naval bases here and overseas.

orld War II took Brunswick permanently out of its Depression doldrums. It also signaled the emergence of Ted Bensinger as a force within the company. Ted's tireless work during the conflict had surprised many Brunswick executives since he had displayed only mild interest in the running of the company before that point.

Ted had joined Brunswick in 1928, a 23-year-old Yale graduate, recently married to Linda Galston, of Woodmere, New York. Like his brother before him, he began work in Muskegon.

Soldiers file into a huge glider for which Brunswick produced parts.

"We honeymooned for nine weeks in Europe. I caught a cold skiing in Switzerland and cured it on the Riviera," Linda Bensinger recalled. "It was glorious. And then we headed straight from the Riviera to Muskegon. It was 20 below when we arrived, and we stayed for two years."

Returning to Chicago in 1930, Ted was elected to Brunswick's Board of Directors, and during the Depression, he moved steadily up the corporate ladder: Assistant Secretary and Assistant Treasurer (1932), General Manager (1936), Executive Vice President (1937). He admitted that, for a time, he was more interested in taking "a lot of little vacations" than looking over ledgers. Those vacations, while they may have irritated some executives, did not bother Ted's brother, Bob. He knew that his family's passions extended beyond the executive office.

Their father, Benjamin, had loved to travel, making plant inspection trips to Europe, and often going to Africa, where he hand-picked ivory for billiard balls. One of his favorite travel stories involved some ivory merchants in Amsterdam.

He went there every year, and was convinced that he was being swindled. The merchants spoke

French and Benjamin decided he would have to learn the language, too. He spent one year taking French lessons and when he returned to Amsterdam, he was ready. He listened calmly as the merchants began raising the bids they were making for him. After a few minutes he called them together and spoke to them calmly for a few minutes in perfect French.

"I was never cheated again," he said proudly.

On many of his overseas trips Benjamin was able to find time for things other than business, and some of Bob's and Ted's earliest memories were set in Europe.

Ted's lifelong fondness for foreign lands and adventure—he took bullfighting lessons in Spain, fished and hunted in the Andes, Alaska, and most places in-between—took a back seat when World War II began. He was very successful in gaining government contracts and became interested in the daily operations of Brunswick. It was as if he suddenly realized that even during war, business was business, and that there existed adventures aplenty in the board room.

Though 1945 marked the end of World War II with such euphoric scenes as this, it was also the year Brunswick celebrated its 100th anniversary, a long way from John Brunswick's cramped Cincinnati woodworking shop.

7 *The Pinsetter Wars*

Stunned by a rival firm's automatic pinsetter, Ted Bensinger works tirelessly to get a Brunswick machine on the market

The first shot in the Great Pinsetter War was fired by the American Machine and Foundry Company in 1946. At the American Bowling Congress tournament in Buffalo, New York, AMF stunned the bowling industry by unveiling an automatic pinsetting machine called the Pinspotter.

Brunswick did little but sit back and wait for the machine to fail. The general consensus in the industry was that it was impossible to create a machine that would pick up pins randomly scattered and put them back where they belonged every time.

As early as 1911, Benjamin Bensinger, his passion for new products and inventors in full flower, had put on the company payroll a Norwegian inventor named Ernest Hedenskoog in hope that he would one day make such a machine. Over the next three decades Hedenskoog managed to fill a Muskegon warehouse with all manner of strange contraptions and a trunkful of patents, but no pinsetter.

Not an inventor in the purest sense, Hedenskoog's desire to create an automatic pinsetting machine resulted from his dislike of pin boys. A precise man and avid bowler, he was forever at odds with them.

The passing of time has endowed pin boys with a charming image. They have become one of

The days of the pin boys, as shown in this 19th century illustration, were about to end as machines began to do most of the work on bowling lanes by the end of the 1950s.

The sport of bowling would never be the same once the world was introduced to Brunswick's Automatic Pinsetter.

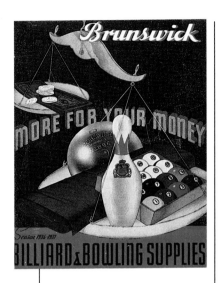

the icons of America's lost innocence. In reality, they were rarely boys, and few were noted for their charm. Their job was tough, backstraining work, an almost constant and dangerous game of tag with flying balls and pins.

"Before World War II," the New York Times reported, "many bowling places had reputations as hangouts for rugged characters who kept the air above the lanes blue with tobacco smoke and rough language; too many pin boys sassed back the customers or heckled the ladies."

Such types did not take lightly to abuse from Hedenskoog and, more often than not, ended his bowling games with fisticuffs. In 1919, he had come up with a magnetic machine able to pick up pins that hid a metal core. But the invention was far from foolproof. So, year after year, decade after decade, Hedenskoog continued to experiment in Muskegon.

Meanwhile, working in a henhouse at a friend's turkey farm in Pearl River, New York, another inventor named Fred Schmidt had developed and patented a vacuum device that seemed to solve the pinsetter puzzle. A jaunty Brunswick salesman named Robert E. Kennedy heard of Schmidt and his machine. Visiting the farm, Kennedy watched with fascination as Schmidt demonstrated his apparatus. On the spot the two men formed a partnership.

Kennedy first approached Brunswick with the project in the late 1930s. He was rebuffed.

"Who needed an automatic pinsetter?," Bob Bensinger re-

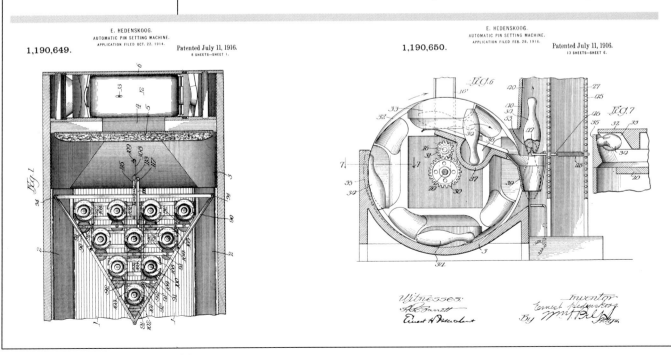

membered. "Not the bowling proprietors—they didn't have the money. Even if they did, why should they buy? There were plenty of pin boys around."

That was a decision he would regret. Kennedy went to AMF with his fistful of patents and a deal was immediately struck. AMF knew machines and sensed the pinsetter's potential. Founded in 1900 by Rufus Lenoir Patterson, the company revolutionized the tobacco industry by developing machines that weighed and bagged tobacco, and rolled and packed cigarettes and cigars. By the late 1930s, as AMF machines churned out a million cigars a year, Patterson's son Morehead was deliberately hunting for products to broaden the company. The automatic pinsetter filled the bill.

Nevertheless, it took AMF more than six years to produce what they believed to be a workable machine. It wasn't. The company's premiere 1946 machines displayed serious defects. They broke down frequently, and in a few months the machines were taken off the market. AMF went back to the research department.

Two years later, when AMF unveiled a second model, Brunswick began to market a semi-automatic device. Again, the AMF machine proved faulty and the company went back to the drawing board. Uneasily aware that AMF's persistence might eventually result in a workable machine, Brunswick hired Huck & Company, a small New York engineering firm, to evaluate all of the pinsetter development Brunswick had done over

Since being put on the company payroll in 1911, inventor Ernest Hedenskoog was determined to create an automatic pinsetting machine. Though his four decades of work failed to produce a practical model, many of his complicated patents provided the basis for what would eventually become Brunswick's Automatic Pinsetter.

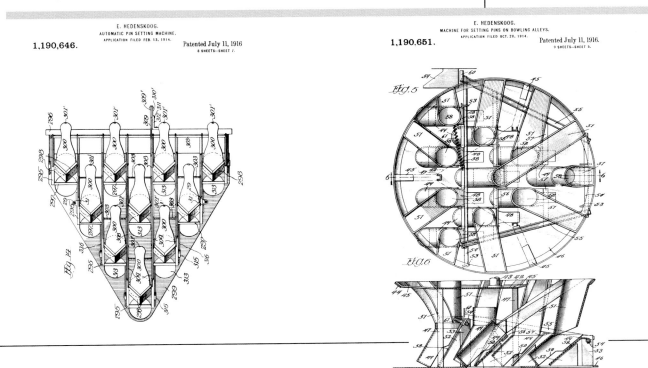

E. HEDENSKOOG.
AUTOMATIC PIN SETTING MACHINE.
APPLICATION FILED FEB. 13, 1914.

1,190,646.

Patented July 11, 1916.
8 SHEETS—SHEET 7.

E. HEDENSKOOG.
MACHINE FOR SETTING PINS ON BOWLING ALLEYS.
APPLICATION FILED OCT. 28, 1914.

1,190,651.

Patented July 11, 1916.
9 SHEETS—SHEET 5.

Brunswick's line of school furniture was a big hit in the nation's classrooms after its 1953 introduction won the company a gold medal from the Industrial Designers Institute.

the years, including Hedenskoog's trunkful of dusty patents.

When Huck reported that Hedenskoog's contributions "contained the nub of a good device," Brunswick gave Huck the go ahead to make a prototype. Brunswick sent one of its employees, an M.I.T. graduate named Saul Jacobson, to New York to handle engineering responsibilities for the project. Unfortunately, money was tight. Though Brunswick's sales were $30.6 million in 1948, the company did not have the funds to

fully bankroll the project and banks were leery of investments in bowling.

The pinsetter project was put on hold while Ted Bensinger concentrated on other fronts. He was named President of the company in 1950 as Bob became Chairman of the Board, filling an office that had been vacant since Benjamin's death in 1935. Ted worked to round up new defense contracts during the Korean War, and he began looking for a new business that would broaden the company's product base. Howard Barber, in charge of corporate sales, was directed to find such products—items that would suit Brunswick's sales organization and manufacturing facilities. He decided on school furniture, and was given $1 million to develop a complete line.

Then AMF dropped a bomb. It displayed its latest Pinspotters in 1952 at Mt. Clemens, Michigan, and they worked.

"When we heard that, it was like a death pall hit the company," recalled a former Brunswick executive. "I was worried. Everyone was worried. I remember asking, 'What the hell are we going to do? Fold up our tents and walk away?'"

Ted Bensinger called Jacobson in New York.

"How long will it take you to get me a workable machine?" he asked.

"If we have the money we need?" said the surprised Jacobson.

"Yes, if you have the money," said Ted.

"I can get one in eight months," said Jacobson.

"Then get started," said Ted, unsure where he would get the many millions it would take to fund the project.

Jacobson and Huck developed a prototype in 1953 but the funds to go into production were still not available. That same year, the company's school furniture line was exhibited with spectacular success. Brunswick's entrance in this new field came at a perfect time, just as the first generation of baby boomers began filling new classrooms. Begun with the 1952 acquisition of Horn Brothers, an Iowa-based manufacturer and distributor of folding bleachers, partitions, and stages for school gymnasiums, this operation was bolstered by the redesign of several products and the addition of a line of classroom furniture designed through consultation with educators, architects, and orthopedic specialists.

The line was exhibited at a 1953 convention of the American Association of School Administrators. It was a smash. Within the year there were 47 exclusive dealers and agents handling customer demand in the United States and Central and South America. The Industrial Designers Institute awarded the new line a gold

medal, the first time it had so honored school furniture.

Bolstered by that success, Ted restructured the company in 1953, forming seven operating divisions: bowling and billiards, school furniture, Horn, defense products, export and subsidiary operations, organization and distribution, industrial relations and personnel. He shifted executives, giving increased responsibilities to many of

This innocent looking member of the first generation of Brunswick's Automatic Pinsetters would not only change the sport of bowling, but alter the face of Brunswick itself.

Anyone who thought Brunswick's first century had been exciting, hadn't seen anything yet, as the success of the Automatic Pinsetter made most past ventures seem tame.

"the bright young men" recruited during the housecleaning of the late 1930s.

Many of them played crucial roles during the Pinsetter Wars. Joseph Stefan aided Bensinger with the complicated legal matters of getting the Pinsetter produced. Lester Swanlund provided financial wizardry. Sid Meyers was tapped to head the bowling and billiards division.

And Ted rallied the troops. "Ted said that if we'd bust our backs and behinds and get in there and scratch, he'd see to it we'd all be well rewarded," Meyers recalled. "All he wanted was miracles."

His energy, however, failed to

impress the bankers, who turned down Brunswick's requests for loans. It was a chance meeting with Byron C. Gould, President of the Murray Corporation of America, that eventually led to the development of Brunswick's Pinsetter.

Murray had just lost a huge body-making contract with Ford Motor Co., and so Gould was in the market for something else. After talking with Ted, a match was struck: Gould had the money, a spare $20 million, and Brunswick had the "something else." Initially, Gould tried to buy Brunswick out of the project for $15 million. Ted would have none of that. Instead he orchestrated a remarkably good deal for his company—Brunswick supplied only the patents to its Pinsetter and Gould supplied $10 million.

"Only Ted's remarkable charm could have swung such a deal," an executive later noted. Others were equally impressed. In what one observer described as a "spontaneous welling up, like at a Quaker meeting," Brunswick's Board of Directors bestowed on Ted in 1954 the new title of Chief Executive Officer.

Brunswick and Murray formed the Pinsetter Corporation. A workable Pinsetter, manufactured by the Otis Elevator Company, was produced within a year and was ready for field testing in 1954. But Murray Corporation's cash involvement began to escalate above original estimates. By the time the

machines were in production in late 1955, Murray had spent nearly $16 million. Gould demanded a renegotiation of the original contract and a bigger share of the revenues.

Ted didn't want that. The only thing he could do was buy Murray out. After a hurried conference with Harold J. Szold, a banker and Brunswick director, Ted approached the C.I.T. Financial Corporation and persuaded it to take a thoughtful look at the Pinsetter's potential. C.I.T. was impressed enough to award Brunswick one of the largest credit lines it had ever extended—$55 million.

Gould, unaware of this transaction, expected to get a bigger share of the pie when he arrived for a meeting with Ted at a Chicago bank.

"It was pure drama on Ted's part," recalled one who was there. "People were squeezed so tight in the room it was hard to breathe and here were all these Murray executives licking their chops at what they thought would be Ted's failure. When he appeared he was smiling like a little kid. He walked over to each of the Murray executives, shaking hands and making small talk. Sticking out of the front pocket of his suit was the end of a check. Finally, when Ted got to Gould, he took the check out and handed it to him. You should have seen Gould's jaw drop."

The check was for $18 million. Murray was out. The Pinsetter was Brunswick's.

8

The Bowling Boom

The spectacular success of the Pinsetter makes bowling a national rage and causes Brunswick's stock to soar

At the end of the 1950s, bowling had firmly captured the fancy of Americans of all ages, a custom-made delight that filled the lanes from coast to coast.

They laughed at us," said Milt Rudo, remembering the reaction of bowling proprietors to the news of Brunswick's Pinsetter. The son of a district manager in Brunswick's bowling operations, Rudo had joined the company in 1940, forsaking Harvard Law School for a career as a bowling salesman. As the Pinsetter Wars heated up, Rudo found himself in charge of 60 salesmen trying to hold the line against AMF's Pinspotter. At first, all they had to offer was Brunswick's reputation and a hastily devised slogan: "Worth Waiting For."

AMF had a huge lead. By the time Brunswick's machine was ready for installation in 1956, more than 9,000 of AMF's Pinspotters had been installed on the country's lanes.

Ironically, the Pinspotter owed much of its early success to Brunswick, which during the 1940s and 1950s had aggressively marketed bowling. It had introduced major design changes, streamlining lanes and adding flashes of color to them. On their way out were the old wooden spectators' benches; they were being replaced with comfortable chairs in a semicircular setting. Brunswick architect Edgar Lynch began designing colorful, cheerful-looking bowling centers.

Often by offering financial aid, Brunswick convinced many bowling proprietors to embrace these

New bowling facilities were popping up all over. For a time it looked like everyone in America was bowling, and those who weren't were busy building new centers.

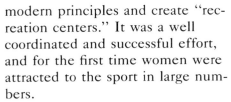

Don Carter and Marion Ladewig display the fruits of a couple of their many victories, providing ample reason why they were the leading members of Brunswick's professional bowling staff.

modern principles and create "recreation centers." It was a well coordinated and successful effort, and for the first time women were attracted to the sport in large numbers.

"Bowling's image was never as bad as that of billiards," recalled Bob Bensinger. "But it needed a little polishing anyway. What we did was bring a more pleasant atmosphere to the sport and women took to it like fish to water."

Women and men alike took to another Brunswick bowling innovation of the 1940s: balls with holes drilled to fit players' hands. These "customized" Mineralite balls were sold in department, jewelry, and even hardware stores. In 1947, the Muskegon plant turned out twice as many as the year before. The company also introduced a lightweight ball called the Junior Mineralite, along with a complete line of accessories for youngsters.

The updating of the sport's gear, the advent of modern interior designs, and the increase in the number of new players convinced many bowling center owners that the sport would grow in popularity. Most everyone, however, was stunned by the explosiveness of that growth. Along came the pinsetters, freeing owners and customers from surly and increasingly hard-to-find pin boys, and allowing centers to operate dozens of lanes at all hours without an army of casual laborers.

And the boom was on.

Sid Meyers had already proven himself in a variety of corporate roles when he was tapped in 1955 to take charge of the company's 125-man salesforce and bring the Pinsetter successfully to market. He had joined the company in 1936 as Credit Manager and became Export Division

Manager in 1939. He became a member of the Board of Directors in 1941, a Corporate Vice President in 1944, and Director of Foreign Operations in 1945.

He was a marketing master, and had to be. He was in a tough and often messy battle, fighting at first a war of words with AMF, which loudly maintained that Brunswick's Pinsetter was beset with problems and would never see market.

He was understandably nervous when, shortly after midnight one night in early April, 1956, four large trucks pulled up in front of the Roselle Lanes, a bowling center in Roselle, New Jersey. Throughout the night and early morning, dozens of workmen unloaded 16 large, cumbersome, and strange looking machines—Brunswick's Automatic Pinsetters.

For the next week workmen toiled furiously to get the machines installed . . . and working. At night, two hulking armed guards watched the premises as if protecting a secret military installation. Such was the bitter nature of the battle with AMF that sabotage was expected.

It had happened earlier in that year. Someone had gotten into the factory where the Pinsetters were being made and snapped pictures of the dismantled machines. One of those pictures found its way to AMF, which sent copies to bowling center owners around the country, accompanied by this pithy note: "This is Brunswick's

Automatic Pinsetter. Are you going to wait for this or buy AMF?"

The wait ended on April 10, 1956, when the Pinsetters made their official debut. It was a major sporting event, covered by dozens of reporters. One wrote in the *New York Journal American:* "With nary a single case of first night jitters, machines on all 16

At an early stage in the production process, here's one of the thousands of Pinsetters that came off the assembly line in Muskegon.

71

These magazine covers perfectly capture the thrills people were getting at their neighborhood bowling centers.

Milton Berle, one of TV's earliest stars, was also one of bowling's biggest boosters.

lanes did exactly what automatic pin-setting machines are supposed to do: they set wood in approved American Bowling Congress fashion, returned balls to their rightful owners, and gave signals via colored lights on an attractive masked unit. All this was done quickly and quietly . . . What more could be asked of a robot—even one that took more than two decades to develop?"

There was little time for jubilation at Brunswick. Of immediate concern was the task of filling more than $30 million in orders. Meyers and his sales team had done a remarkable job. A surprising number of bowling customers believed Brunswick's machine was indeed "worth waiting for." By the night the Pinsetter premiered, orders had already been received for more than 4,000. And at first, production was only a trickle.

"Just as we were all patting each other on the back for holding the line against AMF, we had to figure out how to fill orders for

machines we didn't yet have," recalled Rudo, who worked for Meyers at the time. "Who would we satisfy first? I started getting calls at home from people begging, screaming for their machines. I told them all the truth, that they would have to wait. I was amazed at how many stayed with us. This company had a lot of loyalty."

Loyalty, and a very good product. By the end of 1956, 2,000 Pinsetters had been installed. The next year, that number swelled to 7,000. By 1958 more than 11,000 Pinsetters were doing their work on America's lanes, and the number continued to grow, as if there was no end in sight.

Toward the understanding of the Pinsetter's impact on Brunswick, the following figures speak eloquently.

1954: Sales, $33 million. Earnings, $700,000.

1961: Sales, $422 million. Earnings, $45 million.

The view from company headquarters was stunning. It looked as if everyone in America was bowling, and those who weren't were

busy building bowling centers. Brunswick, determined to solidify its stature in the industry, began to use television, sponsoring "Championship Bowling," a 1950s ratings smash and an effective marketing tool for the sport.

By the thousands Americans were drawn to the sport. In response to this increased demand, new and elegant bowling centers began to dot the suburbs, some costing as much as $2 million. They were air conditioned, with 80 or sometimes as many as 100 lanes. Some had built in restaurants, cocktail lounges, snack bars, and soda fountains, as well as billiard rooms. The more lavish centers offered swimming pools, meeting halls, and nurseries.

These places were called, generically and understandably, "Taj Mahals," but they took such names as Bowleteria, Bowlodrome, Bowlerama, and Bowlero. The largest was Edison Lanes in New Jersey, with 112 lanes side-by-side.

Bowling was fun, healthy, inexpensive, and, to most Americans, novel. Even a beginner could feel the rush of a strike, a brush with perfection. On a subtler level, the centers provided a social focal point for new, sprawling suburban developments.

Behind the scenes with the Pinsetter, these four nuns were captivated by the wonders of the machine.

Everyone wanted in on the action. Gil Hodges, Sherm Lollar, Stan Musial, Joe Garagiola, Yogi Berra, Phil Rizzuto and Mickey Mantle—all of these sports greats, and many others, were proud owners of bowling centers by 1960.

"Perhaps most remarkable is the success of proprietors in luring families into their premises—and the way in which women and children have embraced the sport," noted *Today's Health* magazine at the time. "Women bowlers now number six million (versus 82,000 in 1940), and more than a million of them take the game seriously enough to have joined the Women's International Bowling Congress. The American Junior Bowling Congress has grown from 8,700 boys and girls in 1946 to more than 185,000."

There were more than 100 magazines and newspapers devoted to the sport. Nearly 140 daily newspapers carried bowling columns. Most every metropolitan area had its own local TV bowling program, and bowling stars began to outnumber TV cowboys and private eyes. Brunswick had 60 men and women professionals working for the company and found it necessary to have employees working full-time filling the hundreds of weekly requests for the autographed pictures of such stars as Don Carter and Marion Ladewig's "Bowl to Stay Slim" brochure.

Riding the crest of this boom, Brunswick's stock soared. The company was the darling of Wall Street. Its stock increased spectacularly in value between 1953-59. This naturally thrilled stockholders and the Bensingers, who owned about 10 percent of the company's shares.

Most of the credit for Brunswick's good fortune was showered on Ted Bensinger. He became, to put it mildly, a superstar of the business world, and dozens of national magazines lavished praise on the man and the company.

Fortune, in its November 1959 issue, took a long and detailed look at both in "Brunswick's Automatic Money-Maker." *True* magazine gave them six pages in October 1960: "Ted Bensinger: He Found Profit in Play." *Time* magazine had its say late in 1960: "Ruddy and trim (6 ft., 170 lbs.), Bensinger likes sports and travel

Brunswick aggressively promoted the sport on television and on roadside billboards.

almost as much as his job. He has shot pigeons with Ernest Hemingway in Cuba, sipped wine with Pablo Picasso in Paris, played golf with Sam Snead . . . . He even finds time to bowl occasionally, once rolling a 286 game."

In a profile that makes current sporting-businessmen seem tame by comparison, *Sports Illustrated* devoted five full pages to Ted Bensinger: "The whole Brunswick complex as it exists at present is an extension of one man's astounding energy and drive; it is a monument to Bensinger and the American system of business management—and it is interfering with his duck calling." The December 25, 1961, article—a fine Christmas gift—went on: "Bensinger rides, hunts and fishes. He has fought bulls on Juan Belmonte's ranch and has run with them in Pamplona. He golfs and plays tennis and skis, shoots billiards, bowls, flies airplanes and, of course, calls ducks. In between, he goes to games to watch other people do things."

Ted lived with his wife, Linda, and their three sons, in a large, ivy-covered house in the Chicago suburb of Highland Park. It was there that Linda Bensinger recalled some of the changes wrought by the tremendous success of the Pinsetter. Three decades after the Pinsetter Wars, she sat on the sun porch, a room filled with color that looked out onto the ravine that cut a path through the area.

"There was a time when we had the most wonderful parties here," she said. "We would have all of the employees over. They would fill the lawn." She looked out toward a wide area of grass that stretched into the distance. "It was wonderful. So many nice people and Teddy knew everyone who worked for him. He tried to at least . . . then the company just got so big . . . so fast."

Everybody wanted in on the boom, and New York Yankee great, Mickey Mantle, was all smiles at the opening of his new center.

9 *General Motors of Sports*

Ted Bensinger begins the era of Brunswick's greatest growth by acquiring a number of recreation companies

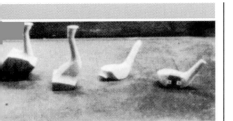

The making of golf clubs became a new part of Brunswick's business in 1958.

Fueled by the success of the Pinsetter, Ted Bensinger developed big dreams for Brunswick, and in 1958, he began to act on them. He would spend the next four years on an incredible buying spree, acquiring 18 new firms of all size and stripe. In the process, he would transform Brunswick.

For more than 110 years, the company's growth had come strictly from internal business development. Bensinger was determined that Brunswick's future growth and diversification would come from acquisitions. Though his dreams would eventually not all come true, his vision took what had been basically a bowling and billiard firm boldly into the new fields that laid the foundation for the company as it is today.

"Ted wanted to make Brunswick into a conglomerate," recalled one executive. "The money generated by the Pinsetters made it easy for him to buy companies. Our stock was so golden that companies were lining up to become part of Brunswick in exchange for stock. Ted was a zealous buyer. It was an exciting time."

Growth through acquisition, though, can be a precarious game. There is no sure thing. Ted played it like a gambler on a hot streak, and he had plenty of backers. To board members and shareholders, Ted had a Midas touch. Most of them considered the success of the Pinsetter his

Union Hardware Company, acquired by Brunswick in 1959, had a long association with American sports, creating such items as this for 19th century skaters.

Zebco would prove to be one of Brunswick's most successful acquisitions, helping fishermen, such as this fellow in the 1980s, catch the big ones.

victory; they credited his enthusiasm and energy with propelling the machine triumphantly to market. So, when he began to expand Brunswick, those around him generally let him have his way.

The most obvious facet of this expansion was Ted's desire to make Brunswick the "General Motors of Sports." He was often heard bouncing that phrase off his executives. They would understand and smile. There was something undeniably catchy about it and the grand idea it implied.

In 1958, Ted began to act, purchasing MacGregor Sports Products Incorporated, a leading

recreational firm that fit his dream to eerie perfection. It had been founded in Dayton, Ohio, in 1834—the year John Brunswick arrived in America. At first MacGregor was in the carriage-making business; Brunswick was a carriage-maker. It took advantage of the late 1800s boom in American participatory sports to enter the golf business, as did Brunswick with bowling. Its headquarters moved to Cincinnati, Brunswick's founding city.

Such coincidences, however, had little to do with Bensinger's decision to buy the company in exchange for $6 million in Brunswick stock. Ted proudly an-

At the MacGregor Factory, the manufacture of golf equipment was an exacting process.

nounced that the acquisition gave Brunswick "the ability to serve the world in year-round recreation."

MacGregor manufactured a wide variety of sporting goods: balls for football, golf, baseball, and basketball; golf clubs, bags, and shoes; shoes and equipment for football and baseball; tennis balls and rackets, as well as gloves and uniforms.

"The purchase seemed like a good thing at first," recalled Joe Donatiello, who started work at MacGregor in 1937, sweeping floors in the shoe factory. "There were some adjustments to be made. But they painted our old factory building, and that was a welcome sign. The place was very old, dark, and dismal. The paint brightened things."

Donatiello was a foreman at the time of the acquisition. Over the next two decades and more he watched MacGregor grow and change, and not always for the best. "We were a family-type place," he said. "We were filled with a lot of old-timers who were used to working on a certain level. Once Brunswick took us over, we started to grow so fast. Old and new methods didn't always work well together. Sometimes they didn't work at all."

Moving further into the recreational field in 1959, Bensinger bought Red Head Brand, a 102-year-old company that was a leading manufacturer of outdoor clothing and equipment in the boating, hunting, fishing, and camping areas. In Red Head's 87,000-square-foot factory on Chicago's Northwest Side, the company also made fishing rod covers, piano and organ covers, voting booth curtains, and, since the 1920s, billiard cue cases for Brunswick.

Union Hardware Company of Connecticut, the world's oldest and largest maker of roller skates, soon joined the fold, along with its line of ice skates, shoes for bowling, football, baseball and track, and golf club shafts. The Royal Manufacturing Company of Ponce, Puerto Rico, also came aboard. Founded in 1952, it manufactured hockey, baseball, boxing, and football equipment.

Almost overnight, Brunswick became a sporting goods giant,

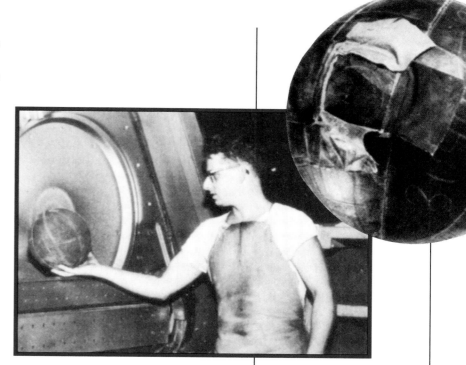

Before bouncing across America, MacGregor basketballs were carefully crafted and built to last.

distributing more than 5,000 products. A new, 166,000-square-foot plant was built in Eminence, Kentucky in 1960 to support and consolidate the manufacture of Brunswick's sporting goods.

Ted kept busy, taking the company into the recreational boating field with the 1960 purchase of the Owens Yacht Company, a leading manufacturer of fiberglass and wooden boats, from 25-foot cruisers to 45-foot yachts. The com-

pany's facility in Baltimore was the largest plant for boat production in the world. Almost simultaneously, Ted bought Larson Boats, a Minnesota manufacturer of small motor boats and canoes.

It was a wonderfully busy period, one that Ted relished. And no more so than on a brisk spring day in 1960 as Brunswick's Annual Stockholders meeting was about to begin at Chicago's South Shore Country Club. Before anyone got down to business, they watched a putting contest between Brunswick directors and professional golfers from MacGregor's advisory staff. This was the sort of flamboyance Ted loved, and that many stockholders expected. The previous year, the shareholder's meeting had been held in a Chicago suburban school to highlight the company's school furniture line.

On the fairways of South Shore's golf course stood such golfing greats as Jack Burke and Louise Suggs, giving a special golf clinic. It was as if Ted and his brother Bob, who remained Chairman of the Board, were trying to provide a physical manifestation of the "General Motors of Sports" dream, something the stockholders could see and feel.

The stockholders were duly impressed: "I'll never forget it," said one stockholder, still wowed after more than two decades. "And you know what? Bob Bensinger hit the ball farther than any of those professionals."

At the massive Owens factory in Baltimore, workers are shown in the process of creating a yacht.

What would prove to be the most important of Ted's recreational acquisitions took place in 1961, when he purchased Zebco. Based in Tulsa, Zebco had begun as the Zero Hour Bomb Company in 1932, making time bombs used to activate oil wells. It was in a different business by the time it caught Bensinger's eye. It had become a leader in the fishing tackle market with a line of closed-face fishing reels.

Zebco's remarkable transformation had taken place in 1949 when a west Texas native named R. D. Hull came looking for work. Instead of a resume, the watch-maker-inventor-fisherman carried in his hands what Harold Binfors, then Zebco's General Manager, referred to as "something that looked like a beer can with a hole in both ends."

The contraption would revolutionize fishing. The sleek Model 22 began rolling off the production line late in 1953, followed soon by the classic Zebco 33. Incorporating the now-famous Zebco contoured thumb button and sensitive drag adjustment, it was America's first true closed-face spinning reel. It was followed by innovations and variations: the 44, made for improved American-type straight handle rods, and the 55, for heavy-duty fresh water fishing, surf casting, and spinning. In 1956, the Zebco name was adopted, and the Zero Hour Bomb Company, still active in the oil field accessory industry, became a division of the tackle firm.

Garbed in nautical attire, Ted Bensinger and Charles Owens happily formalize the deal which made the Owens Yacht Company part of Brunswick in 1960.

Thousands of closed-faced spinning reels rolled off the production line at Zebco's plant in Tulsa.

Ted Bensinger, joined by Japanese Consul General Takeo Ozawa and Mitsui representative Tetsuro Sanda, shares his high hopes for bowling's future in Japan, one of the many foreign countries eager to participate in the sport.

Thanks to the ease with which Zebco products could be used, America started turning on to fishing as never before. Unit sales at Zebco rose a stunning 280 percent from 1954 to 1957. The Tulsa plant expanded as sales and distribution grew from the immediate Tulsa area to embrace all parts of the U. S. and 27 foreign countries.

This spectacular growth did not go unnoticed by Ted Bensinger, a lifelong fisherman. He felt the company a perfect match for Brunswick and he hit it off immediately with Zebco's president, Ralph Lafferty. A charismatic man, Lafferty was revered by many of the employees at Zebco's tidy, homey plant in Oklahoma. He had a personal touch that Ted understood. Walking through the Zebco plant, Lafferty would often stop beside

employee after employee, asking questions such as: "Rosie, how's your little boy?"

Lafferty and Zebco were introduced to Brunswick shareholders at the annual meeting in 1961. Some 5,000 of Brunswick's 75,000 shareholders were on hand, having made their way through the unseasonably snowy April weather to McCormick Place on Chicago's lakefront. They had walked through a lobby filled with 26 luxury yachts and fiberglass boats and displays of other company products. Inside, they sat happily while Bensinger provided a typically upbeat show.

He introduced Lafferty as "the newest addition to the Brunswick executive family." Lafferty's handsome face flashed onto a giant screen on the auditorium stage and the man himself bowed from the audience. Bensinger went on to announce that sales and earnings were going up.

A good portion of the afternoon's program was given to news of the foreign countries in which Brunswick and bowling were making inroads. The shareholders knew that in 1959 Brunswick had purchased a plant near Dublin to manufacture and assemble bowling equipment and that the next year, in partnership with Britain's Rank Organization, 20 movie theaters in England were converted to American-style bowling centers. Ted further informed them of the opening of Brunswick centers in Germany, Holland, Belgium,

The 1961 Brunswick shareholder's meeting had all the style and pizazz of a Broadway show.

France, Austria, Mexico, Peru, Sweden, Brazil, Italy, Switzerland, Finland, and Australia.

The European and Australian markets looked particularly promising for Brunswick and bowling. Few paid much attention to the news that Brunswick had, in 1960, entered the Japanese bowling market through the establishment of Nippon Brunswick, a joint venture in which Brunswick was an equal partner with Mitsui & Co. Ltd., a large Japanese trading company. Few could have anticipated the bowling boom that would eventually seize Japan or the importance of the Southeast Asian market in the coming decades. At the 1961 shareholders' meeting people were convinced that with Ted's leadership, the future would take care of itself.

Ted ended the proceedings with a bang: A 100-foot curtain parted to reveal a newly-designed Owens yacht, shining in floodlights and covered with attractive models in nautical garb. And a band began to play. "It was like a revival meeting or a Broadway opening," recalled one who was there. "It was smiles. It was magic."

10 Into New Fields

Time would prove that Ted Bensinger's entrance into the marine power and medical businesses would be among his wisest decisions

Operating rooms around the world were among the places Sherwood products were found.

The 1961 acquisition of Kiekhaefer-Mercury would surprise even its most optimistic principals.

The appeal of Ted Bensinger's recreational acquisitions was undeniable. They were the most glamorous facet of Brunswick's growth, the most easily grasped component of Ted's dreams.

"Of course, that phrase, 'The General Motors of Sports' is what people grabbed on to," said a former board member. "The recreational acquisitions made good copy for the papers and caused a lot of excitement with stockholders. But Ted's dream was bigger than that, and when you look back, you can see how important some acquisitions in other areas were."

Especially important was the purchase of the A.S. Aloe Com-

pany in 1959, for it put Brunswick into the medical business in a big way. Like Brunswick, Aloe had a long, interesting history. Founded in 1858 by a Scotch-Irish immigrant named Albert S. Aloe, it began as an optical eyeglass shop in St. Louis. As it steadily expanded, its line grew to include cameras, photo equipment, and surgical and surveying implements. Louis Aloe took over after his father's death in 1893, and by the time of the 1903-04 St. Louis World's Fair he was selling such innovative products as microscopes on a time-payment basis, a method then unheard of in the medical business.

Louis Aloe was succeeded by

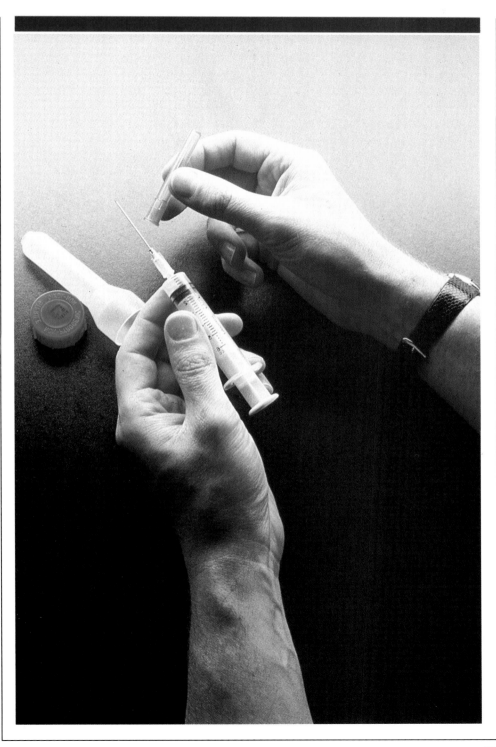

The medical industry appealed to Ted Bensinger for two reasons, its growth potential and its relative stability.

A. S. Aloe founded his company in St. Louis in 1858. When it was purchased by Brunswick in 1959, the A. S. Aloe Company distributed 30,000 medical items through its national catalogue.

Howard F. Baer who was a hunting and fishing acquaintance of Ted Bensinger's. When Ted expressed interest in buying Aloe, negotiations were friendly. The company, which by then distributed a startling 30,000 items through its national catalog, became part of Brunswick for $8.9 million.

With the acquisition of Aloe—along with the addition of the T. J. Noonan Company, Massey Surgical Inc., and Biological Re-

search—Brunswick had one of the nation's largest marketers of hospital and medical equipment. Though Brunswick's medical business began primarily as a distributorship, it wasn't long before Ted started looking for products which his company might not only market but manufacture as well. He found and acquired two such companies in 1961: the Sheridan Catheter and Instrument Corporation, and Roehr Products. Each company was owned by the sort of entrepreneur Ted so strongly admired.

Dave Sheridan, experimenting in a large red barn in Argyle, New York, spent the late 1940s looking for ways to make plastic tubing that would solve the many splicing, sterilization and inventory problems faced by hospitals and scientific laboratories. This tubing was mostly used as catheters, which were used in diagnostic procedures and in introducing and draining fluids from the body.

At the time, catheters were crudely constructed through a means of braiding, varnishing and baking. Sheridan worked for three years to invent a process by which catheters could be made continuously from clear plastic. His method perfected, he turned his barn into a factory and marketed his invention under the "Argyle" brand. His invention rendered old style catheters obsolete.

Equally innovative and successful was the owner of Roehr Products, Matt Roehr, a Polish refugee who had arrived in New York in 1940 with $50 in his pocket. A trained engineer, Roehr was determined to find a new way of making hypodermic needles. He bought a discarded grinder at a junkyard and transformed it into a machine capable of making 300 needles at a time. This method of mass production made disposable needles and syringes feasible. By the time Roehr Products was purchased by Brunswick, the company made 4.5 million needles every week, more than its closest competitor made in a month.

The medical industry was attractive to Ted for two principal reasons: growth potential and relative stability. "Health," he said,

"is as basic to our economy as are recreation, education, and defense. The need for better health care and hospital facilities is being emphasized more and more by local, state, and national governmental agencies as well as by innumerable private interests—thus assuring an expanding market for . . . products and services."

He was right. His medical acquisitions would eventually help the company withstand the financial troubles of the early 1960s and would become the basis for the later formation of Sherwood Medical Industries, the nation's second-largest enterprise in the manufacture, sales, and distribution of medical and laboratory supplies.

Working in a red barn in New York, Dave Sheridan perfected a new way of making catheters, rendering old methods obsolete.

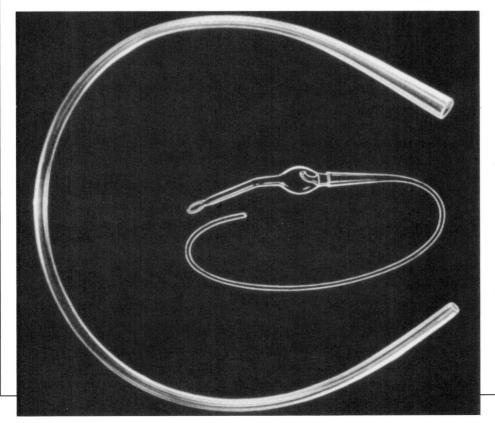

Of all the acquisitions Ted Bensinger would make, none would prove more important than that of the Kiekhaefer Corporation, the manufacturer of Mercury outboard motors.

Like many successful companies, the Kiekhaefer Corporation was a manifestation of one man's dreams and energy. His name was Elmer Carl Kiekhaefer, and he was a tough, strong-willed individualist descended from a family that had farmed Wisconsin land since the 1840s.

As a boy, he preferred tinkering with machinery to plowing, and attended the Milwaukee School of Engineering. In 1939, while working as chief engineer at Milwaukee's Stearns Magnetic Company, he bought a dying outboard motor company near his family's farm in Cedarburg, Wisconsin. With a small crew, he rebuilt the motors left behind by the previous owners. He sold them, and new orders started coming in.

He introduced the Mercury name at the New York Boat Show in the winter of 1939, affixed to motors of both single-cylinder and 2-cylinder alternate-firing designs. These motors incorporated a number of innovative engineering features that were later adopted by the entire outboard industry.

During World War II, when production of outboard motors was halted, Kiekhaefer set out to produce a portable saw for the Army.

E. C. Kiekhaefer, shown here in 1939 overseeing production of his first line of outboard motors, was an engineering genius who helped transform the marine power industry.

It was no simple task. For nearly 20 years, army engineers had tried to develop a portable power saw to replace the heavy, cumbersome models then in use. But in just two months, Kiekhaefer had completed a new machine, and in a test, the saw powered by the Mercury engine cut through a 24-inch green log in 17 seconds, as opposed to 52 seconds for its nearest competitor.

Mercury's design, a 2-cylinder-inline, alternate-firing, air-cooled powerhead of 15-cubic-inch displacement, was accepted by the Army. During the war, the company became a mass producer of such engines, later adding a model with 20-cubic-inch displacement that was rated at 12-horsepower.

At the war's end, Kiekhaefer anticipated an increased demand for larger and more powerful outboard motors. He was bent on expansion, though wartime restrictions on new construction remained in effect. Early in 1946, the newly-formed Association of Commerce of Fond du Lac induced Kiekhaefer to purchase 30 acres of the new industrial park on the southwest side of town. Included in that purchase was a two story barn still filled with 90 tons of hay. One of the handsomest barns in Wisconsin—300 feet long and 50 feet wide—it soon housed 130 Kiekhaefer employees.

The company's expansion perfectly coincided with the growth of the marine industry. Before the war, an outboard motor was mainly

a device to get a fisherman to where the big ones were biting. A six-horsepower motor was regarded as big. But times were changing. With more money and more leisure time, tens of thousands of families were discovering boating. That required bigger boats and larger motors. Water skiing, once deemed a pastime for daredevils, became an important sport, and one that required even greater horsepower.

In 1947 Kiekhaefer introduced the Mercury 10-horsepower Lightning and then moved into higher-powered engines—such as the 40-horsepower, 4-cylinder inline Thunderbolt, the 6-cylinder Mark 75, and others. As the market expanded, so did the company. It built a parts and ser-

Using an engine of Kiekhaefer design, this portable saw amazed the U.S. Army by cutting through this block of wood in 17 seconds. Its nearest competitor took nearly a minute to do the job.

This selection of Mercury motors through the years contains a number of technical innovations that later became standard for the entire marine power industry.

1940	Anti-friction needle bearings on wrist pins
1946	Anti-friction ball and roller bearings throughout
1947	One-piece die-cast aluminum two-cylinder blocks
1949	90-degree consecutive-firing 4-cylinder engines
1949	Four in-line design
1950	Forged aluminum clamp backups
1951	Transom through-bolt provisions in clamp brackets
1952	Impact-absorbing rubber clutch in propeller hub
1952	Automatic tilt-lock for reverse operation
1953	Toothed flexible belt utilized as magneto drive
1953	Production models rated over one hp per cubic inch
1954	12-volt alternator-type direct-drive generator
1954	Key-switch operation of electric starter
1954	Sealed, quick-disconnect remote wiring harness
1955	Sound-absorbent liners for engine covers
1955	1-piece die-cast aluminum 4-cylinder engine blocks
1957	Counter-rotating dual-motor installations
1957	12-volt automotive-type battery ignition system
1957	Single-lever remote throttle and shift control
1957	Propeller torque compensation built into lower unit
1957	Customer propeller choice to suit type of service
1958	Fixed jets replacing adjustable needle valves
1958	Hydraulic shock absorbers for impact protection
1958	Ignition tilt-switch co-acting with shock absorbers

vice division at Beaver Dam, Wisconsin; a boathouse, production plant, and research center at Oshkosh; and new production facilities in Cedarburg and Fond du Lac. From these locations, further innovations poured during the 1950s. The industry's first six-cylinder outboard, the 60-horsepower Mark 75, was unveiled at the 1957 inauguration of the company's Lake "ECK," Florida, proving ground (named in honor of the boss but more commonly referred to as Lake X.)

By 1960, the company had built a large plant at St. Cloud, Florida, for the manufacture of Mercury's line of Quicksilver accessories and aluminum pontoons made of high strength, corrosion resistant aluminum especially suited to salt water use. And that same year announced its first stern drive unit for inboard engines of over 100 horsepower at the Chicago National Boat Show. Named the MerCruiser, the unit offered larger boats the advantages of stern drive, utilizing engineering and safety features introduced on Mercury outboards over the years, coupled with the power and economy of large inboard marine engines.

As a privately held firm, Kiekhaefer Corporation did not publish annual financial statements. But from an initial investment of $53,500 in 1939, revenues had soared yearly. By 1960 industry estimates put the company's sales figure at nearly $50 million. The growth had been tremendous. Distribution was handled through a national network of 3,500 independent dealers. The firm had

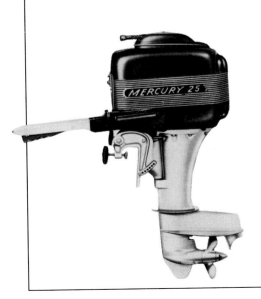

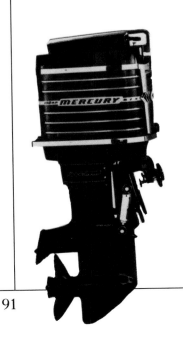

expanded to include plants in six Wisconsin and Florida cities, and three test bases.

But an economic downturn affecting the entire marine industry put Kiekhaefer's company in an increasingly difficult position. In 1961, in order to meet its debt obligations, it would have to go public or answer the calls from Ted Bensinger, eager to make the company part of Brunswick. While the thought of having his company owned by the public was abhorrent to Carl Kiekhaefer, neither was he enthusiastic about joining forces with Brunswick. "He just didn't hit it off with Ted," recalled a Mercury executive.

Kiekhaefer was one of a kind. He owned motorcycles—a 600 BMW, a Suzuki, and several Hondas. He owned cars—a

Lamborghini that he drove from New York to Philadelphia before discovering its fifth gear ("I thought it was revvin' a little high"), a Lincoln, a Cadillac, an Oldsmobile, a Buick, and others. In six years of racing stock and sports cars he excelled, taking three consecutive National Stock Car Championships. His affinity for speed and performance found an outlet too in his company's heavy participation in powerboat racing.

There were dozens of stories about him—racing Ferraris across dirt fields; burying defective cars with earthmovers; ordering Army tanks to patrol his game preserve near Lake X. . . . He had his admirers and some detractors.

"In every sense, Carl thought of the company as his personal property. He had built it and he was not eager to have anyone else poking around, interfering," said a former Brunswick board member. "I think what finally sold Carl was Ted's convincing him he would still run the entire show."

In the summer of 1961 Kiekhaefer sold his company, in exchange for $34 million worth of Brunswick common stock. He became a Brunswick Vice President and joined the Company's Board of Directors. He was, at the time, Brunswick's largest individual stockholder. His firm, he was told, would operate as an autonomous, wholly-owned subsidiary.

"I know Carl had second thoughts about the Brunswick

One can tell from Carl Kiekhaefer's expression that his relationship with Ted Bensinger was far from perfect.

This photo, taken in Mercury's Fond du Lac plant in the early 1960s, barely hints at the division's success.

deal," recalled Bob Anderegg, a former Mercury executive. "I remember the day we signed the papers. It was as if it hit him all of a sudden. The company he built was no longer going to be all his. He didn't want to leave his Chicago hotel room, but finally we went and signed the deal and drove back to Fond du Lac. To Carl, the whole scene was downright depressing."

Whatever Kiekhaefer's feeling at the moment, his company would play an increasingly important role in the company he so reluctantly joined. There was no way of knowing that then. The passage of time is the only way to keep score in the acquisition game. To casual observers, and some financial writers, it often seemed that Ted Bensinger's eyes, so to speak, were bigger than Brunswick's stomach. In some cases they were proven correct. Charting the outcome of Ted's acquisitions is to witness a few corporate shipwrecks amid some spectacular successes.

But as 1961 ended, the future looked full of the prospect of continued prosperity for Brunswick. The number of Brunswick employees had swelled from 5,529 in 1958 to 16,400 in 1961, and the many new companies Ted had gathered into the fold were already making their presence and possibilities felt, cutting into bowling's share of the company's total sales. In 1958, bowling had accounted for more than 75 percent of the company's sales. By 1961, it accounted for less than 60 percent. Even so, the sport was still a huge piece of the corporate pie. But, it was about to crumble.

11 *The Bowling Crash*

The boom goes out of bowling and Ted Bensinger seeks outside help to get Brunswick out of financial trouble

The making of high-performance aircraft radomes would begin to play a more important role in Brunswick's operations during the 1960's.

As faddists and curiosity seekers drifted to other pursuits, many bowling centers had a disturbingly empty look.

Like a nightmare, it began slowly and without obvious pattern. A bowling center proprietor in Ohio was late with a payment for his Pinsetter . . . then another in New York . . . and another in Pennsylvania . . . and another in Ohio.

"No one wanted to believe what we were seeing," recalled Milt Rudo. "At first we just thought these were isolated incidents. Why worry? Bowling was still hot."

A market survey commissioned by Brunswick in 1961 reaffirmed that. The study, which looked at America and bowling on a county-by-county basis, concluded that the end of the bowling boom was nowhere in sight.

"Oh, that survey," said Rudo, rolling his eyes. "It reported that the market could easily absorb 300,000 lanes. This was at a time, remember, when there were only about 125,000 lanes in operation. So, there we were being told that we were just scratching the surface."

Few had expected the sales of Pinsetters and other bowling equipment to maintain their explosive pace forever. A gradual leveling off was anticipated, and even that looked years away. But by early 1962, there was a significant drop in the number of

Where had all the bowlers gone? By 1963, the bowling boom was over.

Citing a fall off in the number of customers, hundreds of bowling center proprietors insisted they could not pay Brunswick the money still owed on its Pinsetters.

bowlers as curiosity seekers and faddists drifted to other pursuits. This tremor was especially alarming to the hundreds of entrepreneurs who had spent and borrowed lavishly to build large, elaborate centers.

During the previous six years, while Brunswick raced with AMF to nail down new territories, the company had eagerly helped fi-

nance centers, often requiring as little as 10 percent down on its then $8,100 Pinsetters and 20-25 percent down on other equipment, with eight years to pay. The risk for proprietors and Brunswick looked rational in the face of blue-sky bowling statistics. But in the period of a few months in 1962, sales of Pinsetters dropped precipitously and hundreds of center owners, citing a fall off in players, insisted they could not meet their payments to Brunswick.

"To put it bluntly, the market had become saturated," said Rudo, who in 1962 was the head of Brunswick's bowling operations. "There had been a tremendous amount of overbuilding. A lot of people went into this business with blinders on, and those people got hurt."

Brunswick, too, began feeling the pain. The company had been borrowing huge amounts of money against future Pinsetter paydays. That was fine as long as Brunswick's customers continued to meet their financial obligations. But as the bowling boom began to go bust in 1962, Brunswick found itself saddled with $359 million in debts to a number of financial institutions. Nevertheless, with new centers closing and bad debts piling higher, the company held to the hope that bowling's downturn was a minor aberration and extended more credit in order to help proprietors.

As the company's financial hole got deeper, a number of bankers, executives and friends began suggesting to Ted that it would be in the company's best interest if he found someone to assist Brunswick in solving its financial difficulties.

"The suggestions were rather subtle at first," said Ed Stephan, a former member of the Board of Directors. "But it didn't take Ted long to realize that he didn't have the financial background to get the company through this crisis. I know that he was reluctant to believe things were ever as bad as the bankers implied. He always

felt bowling would make a quick rebound. But as sales and profits continued to dip, bankers began putting more and more pressure on Ted. Finally he gave in."

The facts were painfully clear. The value of Brunswick's stock dropped from $75 in 1961 to $13 in 1962, and profits plummeted 46 per cent to $24.3 million. By the summer of 1963, Ted arranged a meeting with Jack L. Hanigan, a 52-year-old executive and board member of the Dow Corning Corporation. Hanigan was highly

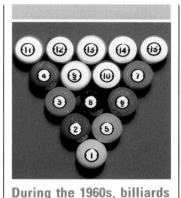

During the 1960s, billiards experienced a renaissance thanks to a film called "The Hustler," starring Paul Newman, Jackie Gleason, Piper Laurie, and George C. Scott. It re-introduced Americans to poolrooms around the country, and new facilities began to go up in suburban shopping centers and middle income neighborhoods. Many of these featured wall-to-wall carpeting, ersatz Tiffany lamps, and pastel tabletops. Most of them featured Brunswick tables. In 1966, some 3,000 new poolrooms opened, the majority called "family billiard centers." Though families sampled, they didn't stay. By 1970, this boom too was bust, and billiards would not again play a major role in Brunswick's operations.

MacGregor was the first choice of discriminating golfers such as young Jack Nicklaus.

regarded by the banking community, and his name was often mentioned when the topic of Brunswick's woes came up. Ted's problem was convincing him to come aboard.

"My initial reaction was not to join Brunswick," Hanigan recalled more than 20 years later, sitting near the swimming pool of his North Palm Beach, Florida home. "A mutual friend set up the meeting between myself and Ted. I liked him a lot, and his company's problems presented some interesting challenges."

The problems in the bowling business understandably overshadowed events taking place in Brunswick's other operations. Though revenues from these divi-

sions were not enough to offset the losses suffered by the bowling business, they did offer some encouraging signs.

In 1963, the School Equipment Division had acquired Burke, Inc., a Dallas-based furniture manufacturer, but nevertheless it experienced a downturn in sales and earnings. The three-year-old International Division realized a small operating profit before taxes; primarily concerned with the sale of bowling equipment in 42 foreign countries, this division was benefitting from the overseas sales of MacGregor golf clubs, balls, and bags.

Sales and earnings in the Defense Products Division showed an increase in 1963. A new plant was

Seemingly at home in this C-5 radome, a Defense Products employee puts a few finishing touches on his day's work.

brought into production in Lincoln, Nebraska to manufacture composite motor cases for rockets and missiles, and the division signed its first contract for the production of the Polaris A-3 second stage motor cases. It continued to be a leader in the field of high-performance aircraft radomes, receiving orders for McDonnell, Grumman, and Lockheed military aircraft.

The Health and Science Division, comprised of seven units—Aloe Medical, Aloe Scientific, Biological Research Inc., Brentwood, Roehr Chemicals Inc., Roehr Products Company Inc, and Sheridan Corporation—showed steady growth. It began selling into such new markets as nursing homes, and added a number of new products, such as diagnostic reagents. By 1963, plans were already underway to market this division's products on an international level.

The recreational businesses, of which the bowling operations were the largest part, was a beehive of various activities. The Bowling Division was marketing its new "A-2" Automatic Pinsetter and promoting bowling with such national programs as "Learn to Bowl" and "League Development."

The Marine Group, which included the Kiekhaefer-Mercury, Concorde (Owens) Yacht, and Zebco divisions, was in especially good shape. Zebco's sales and earnings trend was running seven per cent ahead of that for the overall fishing tackle industry.

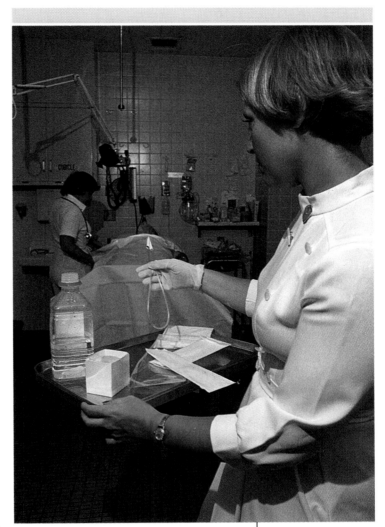

Owens had begun marketing a new line of 32-foot hulls and introduced two new cruisers—the 33-foot fiberglass Sport Fisherman and the 37-foot Express Cruiser. Also within the Recreation business unit, Brunswick's Sports Division—offering MacGregor sporting goods, Canadian Flyer ice

Almost any picture taken in a hospital would contain Sherwood products, such as these catheters.

The hit of 1963: In its first year of marketing, the MerCruiser stern drives became the best selling inboard/outdrive combination in the world.

skates, Union roller skates, Red Head outdoor clothing and life preserver boat cushions—appeared fit.

Kiekhaefer-Mercury registered the highest sales and earnings in its history in 1963. In its first full year of marketing, the new Mer-Cruiser stern drives became the largest selling inboard/outdrive combination in the world. Mer-Cruiser combinations of four-cycle inboard engines and outdrives were thriving; more than 165 boat builders were installing Mer-Cruisers as original equipment on their boats. Sales overseas, through International Mercury Outboards Ltd., maintained an excellent growth rate.

For those who continued to look at Brunswick simply as a bowling firm, the company in 1963 appeared badly bruised and battered.

But for those interested in looking behind the unfortunate situation in the bowling industry, Brunswick was also a company with its fingers in a lot of new and exciting fields. That was what Jack Hanigan was able to see with increasing clarity as he held meetings with Ted Bensinger. And eventually Hanigan made his decision. At a regular meeting of the Board of Directors on November 5, 1963, Hanigan was elected President of Brunswick.

"It is the Board's desire to elect a President who will devote all of his efforts to the effective day-to-day operations, while the Chairman would concentrate on planning for the orderly growth and development of the corporation," Ted announced at the time. "Brunswick is extremely fortunate in securing as outstanding an executive as Mr. Hanigan."

Ted retained his title of Chief Executive Officer and took over as Chairman of the Board. His brother Bob retired from that position, but remained a member of the board, eventually retiring in 1974. This was a difficult time for Ted. In giving up the reins of the company, Ted was forced to accept that for all his visionary skills as a businessman he also had his limitations. And lurking within that was the realization that his decision also ended, but for the relatively short period when H.M. Collender ran the company, nearly 120 years of unbroken family leadership.

Ted was to remain a member of Brunswick's board of directors until 1976. At a formal dinner that year Ed Stephan, a Brunswick Board Member and attorney with Mayer, Brown and Platt, the company's legal counsel since the 1800s, spoke for many when he said, "Ted's style was always informal, flexible, and egalitarian. Some business reporter once wrote that the closest thing to the Brunswick executive offices was a men's locker room, but strangely this was a system in which familiarity did not breed contempt—but rather respect."

Not at all intimidated by the problems caused by the bowling crash, Jack Hanigan became President of Brunswick in 1963 and led the company out of its financial difficulties and boldly into new areas.

In the Fond du Lac factory, a Mercury employee carefully crafts another engine.

I think the whole situation in 1963 came as a terrible shock to Ted," observed Hanigan. "I think he had the feeling that no harm could come to him and his endeavors. The problems his company was experiencing stunned him. I liked him very much. He was a very imaginative guy. And though he was certainly hurt by what had happened, he was by no means a broken man, as I've often read. He was just desperate to get things fixed and he worked like hell with me to do it."

It wasn't easy.

"We had to get tough with our customers," said Hanigan. "I had some fear, at first, that we might not be able to collect the money we were owed. We had to make it clear, in no uncertain terms, that we were willing to take back our equipment if we weren't paid."

It fell to K. Brooks Abernathy to get that money. He had joined Brunswick in 1962 as Assistant Vice President and Credit Manager, after a successful career with General Electric and General Electric Credit Corporation.

"What helped tremendously was the viability of the Pinsetter," Abernathy recalled. "If it was lousy there would have been some defense for non-payment. But it was an excellent machine. We instituted very strong collection methods and the money began to come in. Certainly there were some who couldn't or wouldn't

A few years later executive Jim Urbanek reflected on Ted's contribution: "When the bowling crash came, it obscured everything Ted had done. The same people who had cheered every move he made turned on him, blamed him for our problems. What they never realized was that without Ted's vision and energy the company would never have made it. Sure he bought a lot of companies and most of them helped see us through the hard times. He gave Hanigan a lot to work with."

pay. For them we had only two alternatives: repossess the machines and try to resell them, or operate centers ourselves."

Careful study convinced Hanigan of the latter idea's viability. He believed that professional management could save dozens of troubled bowling centers and offer Brunswick a fighting chance of getting its money back.

Milt Rudo was put in charge of the new Bowling Center Operations Division in 1964, and he organized teams to evaluate centers. More than 300 were assessed and by the end of 1965, the company had taken possession of 131.

"We had no idea how to run them," said Rudo. "All Hanigan said was, 'Do one thing. Don't lose any money.' "

Turning around the bowling centers was but one part of Hanigan's plan to fix Brunswick. Of immediate, if not more complex, concern were the company's dire money matters.

In 1963, the company reported losses of $10 million. The following year it registered a modest $602,000 profit. In 1965, the board of directors set up a $76 million reserve to cover losses and bad debts. Since this loss after audit would have breached major covenants in the company's loan agreements, new loan agreements were signed the following spring. The company also that year received a tax refund of $18 million from the IRS.

In 1966, as Hanigan took over as Chief Executive, the company paid off $66.1 million in debt and reported net earnings of $3.1 million. That summer Hanigan had displayed guarded optimism when he told a group at Harvard, "I am confident that our financial crisis is behind us." But like everyone in the company, he knew there was much work ahead.

The start of something big: Colt Lanes became one of the first properties acquired by the Brunswick Bowling Center Operations Division in 1965.

12 *The Architect of Change*

While finding remedies for the company's financial ills, Jack Hanigan begins to emphasize new fields and markets

The mid-1960s present a dizzying number of corporate alterations—"a change every day," former executive Jack Meyerhoff recalled—as Jack Hanigan began to change the face of Brunswick.

"Hanigan had a clear assignment," said executive Bernie Kornhaber. "It was his job to fix the company, and toward that end he projected total pragmatism. He was going to fix it."

Divisions were born and divisions vanished. Realignments were frequent and sometimes confusing. MacGregor, for instance, appeared in many places on the organizational chart during this period. It was part of Brunswick Sports Division in 1961 (as Brunswick-MacGregor, Inc.), became Mac-Gregor/Brunswick Division in 1965, then part of the Consumer Division in 1966, and the Mac-Gregor Division by 1970.

There was, however, a certain, deliberate pattern to all of this corporate movement. More than anything else it was a manifestation of Hanigan's guiding philosophy, his corporate strategy: "Brunswick must have either a technological edge or a commanding position in the market."

New technologies held great appeal for Hanigan, and one of his most significant actions in positioning the company for future growth was the 1965 formation of a Technical and New Business Division.

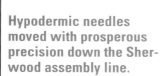

Hypodermic needles moved with prosperous precision down the Sherwood assembly line.

Technical, medical, marine power, and recreation—the businesses of Brunswick are depicted in dramatic sculptural style for the cover of an Annual Report.

Fostered by Hanigan and developed at a cost of $10 million, the company's new metal fiber would prove to have many applications. Among the first was as an addition to carpet fibers to provide anti-static properties.

The division consisted of a research team; a Product Development and Engineering organization; and a New Products unit which was already deeply involved in the pilot production and marketing of Brunsmet, the company's new metal fiber product line. Developed at a cost of $10 million, Brunsmet had many applications. It could be woven together with carpet fiber to provide anti-static properties, or made into an abradable seal for the new generation of high thrust jet engines; it could be used for

sophisticated performance filtration media in aerospace and industry.

It was apparent to Hanigan that such new technologies had applications for the defense industry, and in 1967 the Defense Division and the Technical and New Business Division were incorporated into a Technical Products Division.

The next year, another important change occurred when Hanigan formed Sherwood Medical Industries, Inc., composed primarily of Aloe Medical, Roehr Chemicals, Inc., Roehr Products Company, Inc., Biological Research, Brentwood, Sheridan Corporation, and P.M. Steel Products.

The assets of Aloe Scientific Inc. were sold and at the same time the company discontinued calls on individual physicians by

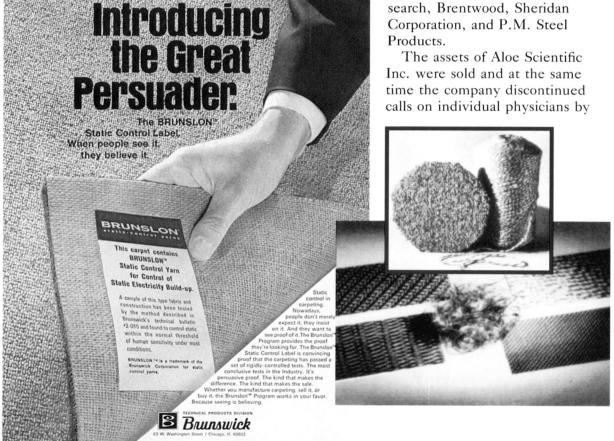

Introducing the Great Persuader.

The BRUNSLON™ Static Control Label. When people see it, they believe it.

This carpet contains BRUNSLON™ Static Control Yarn for Control of Static Electricity Build-up.

A sample of this type fabric and construction has been tested by the method described in Brunswick's technical bulletin #2-015 and found to control static within the normal threshold of human sensitivity under most conditions.

BRUNSLON™ is a trademark of the Brunswick Corporation for static control yarns.

Static control in carpeting. Nowadays, people don't merely expect it, they insist on it. And they want to see proof of it. The Brunslon™ Program provides the proof they're looking for. The Brunslon™ Static Control Label is convincing proof that the carpeting has passed a set of rigidly-controlled tests. The most conclusive tests in the industry. It's persuasive proof. The kind that makes the difference. The kind that makes the sale. Whether you manufacture carpeting, sell it, or buy it, the Brunslon™ Program works in your favor. Because seeing is believing.

TECHNICAL PRODUCTS DIVISION
Brunswick
69 W. Washington Street / Chicago, Ill. 60602

Now, there are 42 carpet makers using Brunslon™ Static Control Yarns in 116 stock lines.

the Aloe sales force. Headed by John N. Willman, Sherwood became a separate company in 1968 when Brunswick sold a 15 per cent stock interest to the public. Sherwood made and marketed more than 30 brand names—including industry leaders Monoject, Lancer, and Citadel.

"This represented an important strategic thrust," said Meyerhoff. "Hanigan wisely determined that we should be distributing only products we made. It gave us greater control and efficiency. It was a master stroke."

Nineteen sixty-eight also held a pleasant surprise: the Bowling Center Operations Division started turning a profit. It wasn't easy. Winning the confidence of other center owners had been difficult. At first they were reluctant to believe the "we're all in this together" spirit Brunswick tried to foster. Times were tough and words did not speak louder than what some owners interpreted as unfair encroachment. But the company did more than talk. It became point man in the effort to stabilize the bowling industry. Commissioning studies, reports, and surveys, Brunswick shared all of its research with other owners and the media.

What made Hanigan's corporate life considerably easier during the mid-1960s was the spectacular growth of Mercury. In 1964, when Mercury celebrated its 25th anniversary, ground was broken on the first phase of a multi-million dollar

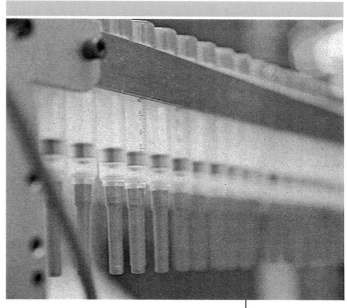

expansion of the facilities in Fond du Lac, Wisconsin. The following year it experienced tremendous growth in Canada. The international market in general was enthusiastic about the company's economical 60-horsepower Mer-Cruiser 60.

In 1966 Mercury introduced the 110-hp Merc 1000SS, the most powerful outboard ever built, and followed that in 1968 with an even more powerful 125-hp engine. These important innovations coincided with the second major phase of Mercury's $9 million expansion program—the construction of another 370,000 feet of plant area in Fond du Lac. The new buildings included an engineering center, a heat treating plant, and a giant fa-

Sherwood's Monoject line of disposable needles and syringes—a leading choice of doctors and hospitals.

A Mercury motor was a sophisticated piece of machinery that went through dozens of production steps before hitting the world's waters.

cility consolidating assembly, paint, and test operations. Construction also began on a manufacturing and assembly facility outside Melbourne, Australia.

Led by the indomitable Kiekhaefer, Mercury thrived. Its sales figures more than doubled between 1961 and 1969, when they topped $135 million. "Many of Carl's contributions have been buried by the years," said former Mercury executive Bob Anderegg. "He was a genius with machinery, and the growth of Mercury, especially during the 1960s, was the result of his determination and desire for constant improvement in

our products, and his ability to give real life to his dreams. When Carl Kiekhaefer had an idea, it usually changed the face of the industry."

There is no way to underestimate Kiekhaefer's success with Mercury or his influence on the marine power industry. But as Mercury grew to become a larger part of the Brunswick corporate pie, so its day-to-day operations attracted greater attention from corporate headquarters. This put an increasing strain on the relationship with Kiekhaefer.

"Carl thought he could run the whole operation from his desk," recalled Anderegg. "But the growth was so dramatic. I'm sure he saw the handwriting on the wall. In a way he was like Ted Bensinger—a victim of his own success. One way or another he knew that he would have to give up the company. It was no longer the kind of place that could be run as a one man show." And so, in 1969, K. Brooks Abernathy took over the presidency of Mercury from Kiekhaefer.

Late in 1970, Newsweek magazine sent a reporter to the company's headquarters on Washington Street in Chicago. What he found was a company vastly different from what it had been but a decade before. The reporter met with Hanigan, who had just returned from a trip to Japan for the opening of a sports complex that

included bowling, billiards, and indoor golf; part of the joint venture between Brunswick and Mitsui called Nippon Brunswick.

The two men talked for an hour. Hanigan spoke deliberately when discussing some of the changes that had taken place in recent years: the closing of the company's bowling centers in Australia in 1966, and the closing of a factory and more centers in Italy; the selling of Red Head in 1968, the 1970 sale of (Owens) Concorde, and the sale of the school furniture line in 1969.

Hanigan was more animated when talking about Brunswick's first major acquisition since the early 1960s—Sherwood had that week agreed to buy Pioneer Rubber Co., a maker of gloves for the

medical, surgical, and industrial fields, as well as promotional balloons. And he was especially proud and eager to discuss Brunswick's sales in 1969: $450 million, which topped the company's previous record, 1961's $422 million.

"This is a whole new company," Hanigan told the reporter. "Brunswick is a company that just happened in the last 15 years."

Indeed. In 1955, Brunswick had been a relatively small bowling and billiard company struggling to get an automatic pinsetter to market. By 1970, through boom and bust, it had become less recognizable as a bowling company. With its new emphasis on the medical and technical fields just starting to be felt, Brunswick was presenting a picture of growth and stability

When bowling boomed in Japan, it wasn't unusual to see people stopping on their way to and from work to bowl a few lines.

The hugely successful MerCruiser is shown in close-up and moving along the assembly line in Fond du Lac.

that the financial community was finding very encouraging and attractive.

Nowhere were things brighter than at Mercury, where sales increased from $150.4 million in 1970 to $267.9 million by 1973. But late that year, the Arab oil embargo and the ensuing energy crisis threatened future sales. Instead of getting edgy, the company quickly moved to position itself for inevitable recovery. An eight-acre parts center was built at Fond du Lac in 1974. It was computer controlled and shipped

products to 128 countries. With energy costs and supplies utmost in mind, Mercury revamped its motor line, from the 175-horsepower Black Max to the 4-horsepower Gnat. New carburetor design and other engineering improvements made significant gains in fuel economy for Mercury outboards. And, in 1974, ground was broken for new manufacturing facilities in Stillwater, Oklahoma.

The recession affected the entire company. In 1974 earnings dipped slightly, after eight consecutive years of increases. Reacting to this, Hanigan and K. Brooks Abernathy, who had become President of Brunswick in 1972, began a reorganization of the company into four business groups—Medical, Technical, Marine Power and Recreation—with a number of divisions within each of them. It was their desire to eventually grow each of these divisions into equal parts of the corporation's revenues—a sturdy four-legged corporate stool, if you will—thereby allowing the entire company to better withstand the sour economic times to which all recreational businesses were vulnerable.

This vulnerability had just been on dramatic display in Japan, where bowling was playing out an interesting, if frighteningly familiar, scenario. Though there were only some 500 bowling lanes in Japan during most of the 1960s, late in that decade bowling fever hit the country. People could be seen

carrying their bowling balls to work, often stopping for a few games in the morning and returning after work, sometimes bowling until midnight. To meet the demand, centers began to rise throughout the country, lavish centers with 50, 60, or more lanes.

And then, mirroring the sport's misadventures in America, it all fell apart. From 130,000 lanes installed in 1973, only 27,000 were built the next year. Corporate net sales of bowling products to Nippon Brunswick plummeted from $64 million in 1973 to $1 million the following year.

Fortunately, the company's other international ventures were not experiencing such trauma. Especially important was what was taking place with Mercury.

Mercury's first European plant at Petit-Rechain, Belgium, began producing outboard motors in 1972. Mercury also built a fully-equipped distribution center and training and service center on the Meuse River in Belgium as a supportive facility to the production plant. And Europe wasn't the only foreign locale where Mercury was growing. Canadian assembly operations moved from Toronto into a new home in Mississauga, Ontario.

What would prove a major strategic decision took place in 1972 with the formation of a joint venture with the Japanese firm Yamaha. This venture, called Sanshin and started by Abernathy, was an agreement to produce and market a new line of outboards.

Bowling comes to Moscow, and this announcement heralds the 1976 opening of a 16-lane Brunswick center.

Brunswick's expertise at making sophisticated radomes resulted in increasingly larger contracts.

One of the most crucial players in this venture was Jack Reichert, who was named president of Mercury that same year. A native of West Allis, Wisconsin, Reichert joined Brunswick in 1957, a 26-year-old who had worked in a variety of marketing positions for General Electric. After coming to Brunswick, he worked in the bowling division for 14 years, eventually rising to Vice President for Marketing. In 1971, he arrived in Fond du Lac for a similar position with Mercury. When Abernathy moved down to Skokie to become Brunswick President, Reichert took over as President of Mercury and became the leading force in the eventual Sanshin success.

Sanshin would produce a line of outboards for Yamaha under the name of Yamaha and for Brunswick under the name Mariner. Sanshin-produced engines for Yamaha and Mariner brand names, at a given horsepower, were the same engines. Yamaha would sell Sanshin-produced engines under the Yamaha name in Japan, while Brunswick would sell Sanshin-produced engines under the Mariner name.

Built up to 55 horsepower, Mariner outboards were produced in Japan and first introduced in 1974 in Australia. Initially marketed in that country, New Zealand, Latin America, Southeast Asia, and Europe, this new line enabled the Marine Power Group to strengthen its competitive position on an international level.

The importance of this strategy was that it essentially gave the company a second line of outboards. Mariner was able to penetrate markets that Mercury could not.

And there was increased activity on other fronts as the company's technical businesses grew dramatically during Hanigan's tenure. Thanks to his determined nurturing, Brunswick laboratories put the corporation into new businesses. The Defense Division not only was turning out radomes and transportable shelters, but also, thanks to its increasing innovations with metal fibers, camouflage for the U.S. Army.

Though Hanigan retired as Chairman and CEO in 1976, he remained on the Board of Directors and watched as his faith in new technologies continued to benefit the company he helped transform.

"There were a lot of crucial moves. Some worked. Some didn't," Hanigan recalled. "My goal when I came to Brunswick was to get things fixed, to fix the things we had and make them profitable. And to build on what we had. We could build on Mercury and the medical businesses. Before I came aboard there was little emphasis on research and development, on new technologies. I changed that . . . . Oh, it was a hell of a good time. I always thought there was light at the end of the tunnel. I'm just glad I was able to help find it."

Final assembly checks are conducted on an antenna reflector which would soon become part of a tactical radar system produced by the Defense Division.

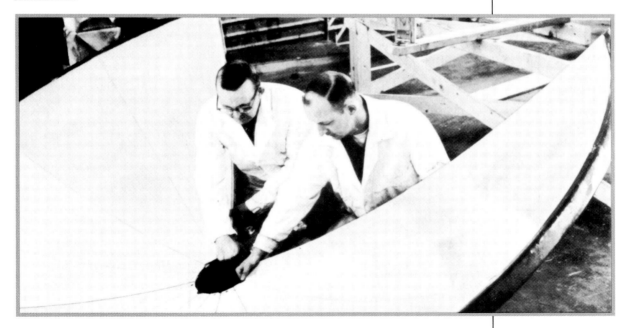

13 *An Orchestrated Growth*

K. Brooks Abernathy was determined that Brunswick continue to concentrate on new technologies, such as those with applications in the medical industry.

Brooks Abernathy brings increased organization to the company as he prepares to capitalize on and build Brunswick's technical businesses

An environment for results." That was what K. Brooks Abernathy was determined to create when he became Chairman and CEO of Brunswick in 1976. In the late spring of that year he set forth, in very concrete terms, what he considered his mission.

"Our goal is to establish an environment which is oriented toward results, along with the freedom of initiative and a capacity for calculated risk-taking," he said. "We will do those things we can do well and profitably. We will seek areas where we have unique abilities and strengths in product invention, in process improve-

ment, in production techniques, or market experience or expertise."

Like Hanigan before him, Abernathy was determined that Brunswick have greater stability than could be provided by relying so heavily on what he called "the volatile and precarious recreational fields." That meant further strengthening the company's medical businesses and greatly expanding the company's technical ones.

The structure instituted two years before when the company was organized into four business groups—Marine, Medical, Recreation and Technical—was

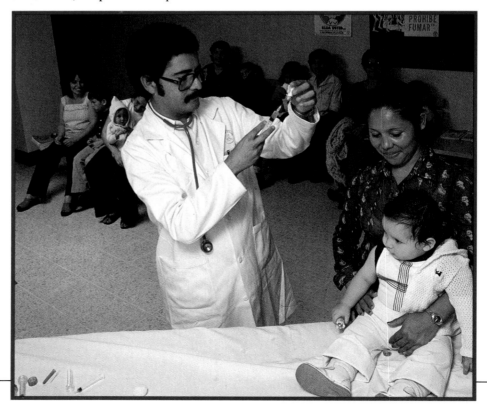

Brunswick products could be found working in a number of new fields during the late 1970s, such as here at an oil pumping station in Texas.

completed in 1976, and Abernathy deemed it essential "to accommodate the growth ahead." The next year Abernathy brought Jack Reichert from Fond du Lac to become Brunswick's President and Chief Operating Officer.

"I had really enjoyed working at Mercury," Reichert recalled. "I was so happy in Fond du Lac that initially I was reluctant to even leave."

Growth appeared certain. The company was rebounding nicely from the economic recession of 1975, which had been compounded by a seven-week strike at Mercury. By 1977, the company, with more than 25,000 employees, topped $1 billion in sales for the first time. Organization and planning were essential.

"Brooks was determined to conserve the gains the company had made. They had been very hard won," said executive Bernie Kornhaber. "He wanted to build slowly and conservatively. He wanted the company's progress to be formalized, well orchestrated, planned to the smallest details. With the bottom line always in mind, he never jumped feet first."

Sherwood was playing an increasingly important role, experiencing steady internal growth, supplemented by careful expansion. It was apparent that the operation's manufactured items were more profitable than others which it only distributed. As a result, in 1978 the Aloe medical resale and distribution business was discontinued, and greater focus was given to manufacture of disposable medical items.

Monoject needles and syringes filled the supply shelves of hospitals and were the first choice among dentists and veterinarians. The Argyle Division manufactured more than 100 types of medical tubing, and the Lancer Division was adding to its line of supplies for clinical laboratories, expanding

The large Continuous Polymer Filtration unit (below) and a number of other filters (inset) played important roles in Brunswick's success on the technical front.

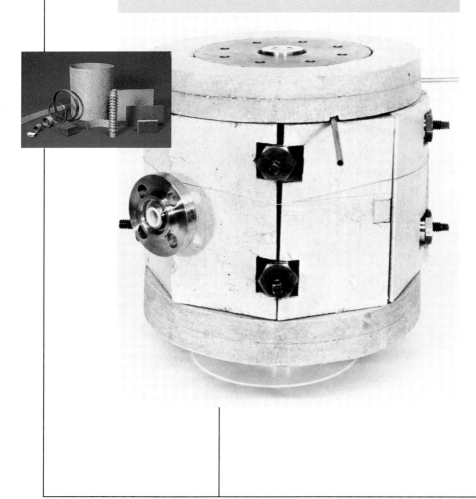

from disposable products to diagnostic items. As diagnostic testing grew in sophistication, Lancer was at the forefront, also becoming a leader in the sale of liquid handling devices, tissue embedding media, and glucose tolerance beverages.

The Technical Group, which Abernathy called "our fastest growing area" in the mid-1970s, included the Defense and Technetics Divisions. It produced a complicated, though increasingly prosperous, collection of high tech products that had a variety of uses in many fields.

"We had a good start in our technical divisions," Abernathy said. "We were in many highly fragmented businesses. We worked to find niches where we could."

In 1976, the Defense Division acquired certain assets of Celesco Industries, Inc. of Costa Mesa, California. That facility was given the responsibility as the division's engineering center with the primary function of developing new business and technology. The unit produced the boom arm on the Viking Mars Lander. While the Defense Division continued to turn out such products as radomes for military aircraft, composite motor cases for missiles and rockets, and a variety of transportable shelters, perhaps the group's most exciting new developments involved the use of Brunswick's metal fiber technology.

The fibers, born of Brunswick research in the 1960s, were being used to make a new lightweight camouflage net in various color combinations for the U.S. Army; it not only fooled the eye but also radar and infrared cameras. It was being assembled at both the Division's DeLand, Florida, facility as well as at the Devils Lake Sioux Manufacturing Corp., a joint ven-

Building transportable shelters for Army field hospitals like the MUST became an increasingly important part of the Defense Division.

ture owned by Brunswick and the Sioux Tribe of Devils Lake, North Dakota. As well, the metal fiber product was also being used extensively as a jet engine seal and acoustical dampener for the Technetics Division.

Technetics was growing in the filtration business. Two Brunswick companies acquired in the early 1970s, Fluid Dynamics and Filterite, were providing a vast number of filters utilizing materials from stainless steel fibers to cotton, to a number of industries.

"What we were doing was looking for unique products," Abernathy said. "Something we could bring to the marketplace that was not already there. Those were our niches."

Amid this group's prosperity there was one sour note. It involved Ozite, a Chicago maker of indoor/outdoor carpeting, that Brunswick had purchased in 1974 for $14 million. The success of Brunsmet metal fibers in the manufacture of static-free carpeting had convinced Hanigan to take the company more determinedly into that business. It didn't work, and Abernathy was forced to sell Ozite in 1979.

Brunswick's homegrown Defense Division became a leading producer of new lightweight camouflage net for the U.S. Army.

That minor failure impeded not at all the company's growth. In 1977, Brunswick acquired Circle Seal of Costa Mesa, California. It became part of the Technetics Division along with its product line consisting of thousands of valves, regulators, and controls used in a variety of industries: defense, aerospace, maritime, chemical, energy, heavy machinery, and life-support.

Abernathy boldly moved Brunswick into such new fields as energy and transportation with an acquisition that took place the next year, with the purchase of the Vapor Corporation. At $90 million, it was the most expensive purchase thus far in the company's history.

Founded in 1904 by Egbert H. Gold as the Chicago Car Heating & Lighting Company, it was one of the country's leading manufacturers of heating systems for railway cars. Its first customer was the New York Central, followed by the Union Pacific, Burlington

and Quincy, Illinois Central, and Sante Fe lines. Its equipment was standard on Pullman cars.

Vapor had proven itself especially adept at tailoring its own growth and operations to the rapidly changing needs of the transportation industry in the U.S. and in Canada, through its subsidiary Vapor-Canada. It had also made inroads in the energy field. When acquired by Brunswick, Vapor was making door opening systems, fare collection boxes, climate control systems, relays, speed indicators, steam generators,

With the purchase of the Vapor Corporation, a firm originally known as the Chicago Car Heating & Lighting Company (picture at left), Brunswick was into the energy business with Vapor's line of valves, shown below.

electric boilers, thermal storage equipment, tank gauges and fittings, chemical injector pumps, valve actuators, process control products, and plug, safety, and relief valves.

Vapor's sales at that time exceeded those of either the Defense and Technetics Divisions, and it was designated a separate division within the Technical Group.

While that group expanded, the Recreation Group became leaner. During the late 1970s, Abernathy sold off the marginally profitable but unpredictable golf, basketball,

baseball, skiing, and archery equipment businesses to a number of different companies. The Brunswick Recreation Centers Division operated more than 250 bowling centers worldwide and provided welcome cash flow. The Brunswick Division continued to produce bowling and billiard equipment at a profit, introducing the revolutionary Systems 2000 laminated bowling surface to replace older wooden lanes.

Zebco, a separate division within the Recreation Group, could boast through the mid-1970s that more than 60 per cent of all

A perfect day for fishing: A man, his boat, and his Zebco reel.

spin-cast reels purchased in the United States bore the Zebco name.

The Marine Power Group had proven remarkably adept at dealing with the precarious American economy. MerCruiser had become the group's fastest growing division, soaring to record sales after the introduction of its aluminum block engine in 1976, the first die-cast engine designed specifically for stern drive use.

The Mariner Division, which introduced its outboards in North America in 1976, showed continued expansion as it added dealers and distributors to its network, and consumer acceptance of the Mariner line increased. The Mercury Outboard Division, continuing to emphasize fuel efficiency, increased its sales as well, particularly in Mexico, the Middle East, and Europe.

The Marine Power Group set sales records throughout the 1970s. Its first decline came in 1980 when it felt the effects of the economic recession brought about by another oil shock that affected the entire American economy. Added to that was a proposed government ban on weekend boating, which fortunately was never implemented. By initiating a number of cost cutting programs, including the expansion of a plant in Mexico, the Group experienced a very positive turn-around in operating earnings in 1981, an upswing of more than $50 million over the previous year.

Indeed, the brighter economic

climate made 1981 a record year for Brunswick. Abernathy's faith in the health and technical fields was paying off. Those businesses, which had accounted for 33 percent of sales and 29 percent of earnings in 1976, had risen to 50 and 66 percent respectively by 1981.

Since 1970, Brunswick's sales in the U.S. had grown an impressive 125 percent, to $1.1 billion. International sales had soared, increasing by 460 percent in the decade, accounting for more than 26 percent of the company's total revenue. Earnings for 1981 were a record $66 million.

Brunswick's new and increasingly prosperous look began to attract a lot of investor interest. Many Wall Street analysts thought Brunswick vulnerable for a take-over attempt.

Brooks Abernathy, shown here at the Great Wall during a visit to China, would be a driving force behind Brunswick's international expansion.

"When you looked at the stock price in relation to the book value," said one analyst, "you could see that the company's pieces were worth more than the whole pie. And that's the kind of thing that makes a pretty takeover picture."

The products and people of Sherwood, here represented by a lab technician and a colorful panorama of its needles and syringes, began to attract the interest of some take-over minded companies.

January 24, 1982. Abernathy was sitting in the living room of his suburban Chicago home, watching the tail end of the Super Bowl game between the Cincinnati Bengals and the San Francisco 49ers, when the telephone rang. On the other end was Joseph Albrandi, president of Whittaker Corporation, a Los Angeles-based conglomerate. In a brusque manner he announced to Abernathy that Whittaker would attempt to buy Brunswick.

A messenger arrived at Abernathy's home within the hour, carrying the details of Whittaker's deal. It was offering $26.50 a share for 10.4 million of the outstanding Brunswick shares, plus an offer to

buy $30 million in convertible debentures. If successful, Whittaker would control 49 percent of Brunswick's voting stock.

"I was angry," Abernathy recalled. "I was surprised by the aggressive nature of the offer. It was very sudden and unfair."

By the following morning, board members and executives were gathering at corporate headquarters in Skokie. They did not take kindly to the offer and, at a special board meeting three days after Super Bowl Sunday, the company turned down Whittaker's offer and decided to fight the takeover. It would be a bloody battle.

"The board was concerned that the transaction was unfair to share-holders, and that the quality of the non-cash portion was questionable," Abernathy said. "As well, Whittaker's ability to meet its debt obligations was suspect because the majority of its earnings came from its medical businesses in the volatile Middle East."

It was obvious what Whittaker wanted most from Brunswick: Sherwood. That purchase would provide it with the sort of broad-based, international medical manufacturing business needed to balance its medical distribution business, and thus make it more competitive with firms like American Hospital Supply.

Brunswick brought a lawsuit against Whittaker on the grounds of anti-trust violations and the unfairness of its proposed transaction. The nature of the proposed package indicated that Whittaker would be forced to sell various pieces of the company in order to fulfill its debt obligations while trying to hang on to Sherwood.

That scenario was most distasteful for Brunswick. A "white knight," a friendly company that might purchase a controlling interest of Brunswick and thus thwart Whittaker, could not be found. "A lot of companies were interested in buying parts of us," said a board member. "What most seemed to want was the medical business."

A deal was struck by which American Home Products Corporation would acquire Sherwood in a stock swap arrangement. In the deal, American Home Products invited Brunswick shareholders to

sell their shares at $30 each, up to a maximum of 14.2 of the 26 million shares outstanding. American Home Products would then exchange the block for all of the shares of Sherwood, a wholly owned subsidiary.

"The move seemed highly beneficial to both Brunswick and American Home, a big manufacturer of drugs and household items," reported the New York Times during the transaction. "Assuming the deal went through, not only would it deprive Whittaker, a company with interests in box cars, chemicals, and health care, of Brunswick's key Sherwood operation, but also would have sharply reduced outstanding shares. This, in turn, would increase earnings per share on Brunswick's remaining operations."

On March 8, Whittaker withdrew its offer. The following day Sherwood was disposed of for 14.2 million shares of Brunswick stock that American Home Products had received through its tender offer. The deal amounted to $425 million.

The transaction, however, did not sit well with some. Some Sherwood employees felt "like a child who had just been abandoned by its parents." Other critics denounced the deal as "selling the crown jewels" and questioned the performance of the board during the takeover battle.

"It took a lot of strength to make this decision," Reichert remembered. "The Board

Newspaper headlines boldly chronicled the battle for survival that Brunswick successfully waged against the takeover minded Whittaker Corporation.

Sun-Times, Thursday, February 25, 1982   business

Whittaker extends offer to buy Brunswick shares

Whittaker Corp. said it is extending its offer to buy Brunswick Corp.'s securities to March 12 from its original date of Feb. 26. Meanwhile, Whittaker said a federal court here is expected to rule Thursday on its motion to have Brunswick's proposed sale of its Sherwood Medical unit to American Home Products declared illegal. Brunswick, meanwhile, said it is confident it will be able to move forward with the sale. Separately, several analysts say that Brunwick "will lose its attractiveness" if it sells Sherwood, the "fastest growing, highest profit" sector of Brunswick's business.

(composed of Abernathy, Sidney Davidson, Hanigan, George D. Kennedy, Ian MacGregor, Charles P. Neidig, Robert N. Rasmus, J. Donald Rauth, Reichert, Pierre Rinfret, John T. Rettaliata, and Ed Stephan) knew that we'd be ripped to pieces. Few really understood all the complexities of the situation. This was the most critical period in the company's history and the board acted with remarkable courage."

Later in March, Brunswick announced that it would be forced to reduce its corporate staff by one-third. Though the company provided additional special benefits for departing employees, it was not a pleasant scene in Skokie, even for some of the survivors.

"It was terribly sad," said one who remains with the company. "None of us really knew what to expect. There was such a sense of uncertainty. Were we going to get pink slips in our last payroll envelopes?"

"Though I was elated that the company was able to survive," Abernathy said, "the immediate impact was most unpleasant. Many people were hurt."

In what the Chicago Tribune characterized as a "surprise move," Abernathy announced at the annual stockholders meeting in April, 1982, that Jack Reichert would take over as Chief Executive Officer of Brunswick.

THE NEW YORK TIMES, FRIDAY, JANUARY 29, 1982

Market Place / Robert Metz

Whittaker Bid For Brunswick

THE Whittaker Corporation's efforts to acquire the Brunswick Corporation might seem counterproductive to people who admire the way Whittaker has streamlined its operations by getting rid of 89 businesses. Whi...

THE WALL STREET JOURNAL,
Monday, March 8, 1982

Brunswick Says Court Backs Ruling to Allow Sale of Its Medical Unit

By a WALL STREET JOURNAL Staff Reporter
SKOKIE, Ill.—Brunswick Corp. said a U.S. appeals court upheld a lower court decision lett... ll its Sherwood Medical Home Products

THE WALL STREET
Friday, February

Brunswick C Whittaker Ea A Round in Co

By a WALL STREET JOURNAL Staff
CHICAGO—A federal judge re enjoin Brunswick Corp. from se Sherwood Medical unit to American Products Corp. But he also declined wick's request that Whittaker Corp stopped from proceeding with its tende fer for 10.4 million Brunswick shares.

Chicago Sun-Times, Tuesday, March 9, 1982 | business

Whittaker drops takeover offer

Whittaker Corp. terminated its tender offer for a 49 percent interest in Brunswick Corp., citing its unsuccessful efforts to prevent Brunswick from selling its Sherwood Medical subsidiary to American Home Products. The U.S. Court of Appeals for the 7th District Friday denied Whittaker's request for a preliminary injunction against the sale. Whittaker said it will return all Brunswick securities tendered to it as promptly as possible. American Home will start purchasing tendered Brunswick stock Tuesday under its $30-a-share offer for 14 million shares. The offer's withdrawal period expired Monday and the proration period expired Feb. 25. Because of the amount of Brunswick stock tendered before the proration date, American said it does not anticipate buying any shares tendered after Feb. 25.

14 Into High Gear

Rebounding from the effects of a spirited takeover battle, Jack Reichert puts bold, new plans into action.

Abradable seals made by Technetics are an essential component of many jet engines.

After he became Chief Executive Officer of Brunswick, Jack Reichert was offered a lot of advice.

"Get rid of Mercury and all the other recreational businesses," he was told. "Concentrate on the technical end of Brunswick."

Reichert listened. He didn't like what he heard and rejected the advice. "People were telling me that Sherwood had been our only good operation," Reichert said. "And that made me angry. I couldn't accept that opinion. Because of the trauma of the time—there's no doubt that Brunswick was an injured company—many people lost sight of the fact that we were in good businesses, and had leadership positions in most of them."

Reichert was determined. On many nights he sat up making plans, writing down his goals and expectations for the company. His predecessors had left him with a solid company, he felt, but it was a company that needed to change, and change quickly and dramatically if it was to overcome the effects of Whittaker's takeover attempt and the disposition of Sherwood.

"A lot of people don't understand numbers. But everyone understands values," said Jack Reichert, shortly after becoming Brunswick's Chief Executive Officer.

The powerful engines of Mercury, the largest marine engine business in the world, being tested at its MerCabo facility in Placida, Florida.

It was his belief that by decentralizing the company he could ensure greater efficiency and response time. He was also determined to divest those businesses in which the company, for one reason or another, could not be in a leadership position; to retain and fix Brunswick businesses which needed fixing; to introduce new technologies through venturing, and to enhance the growth of existing businesses through acquisitions.

It was a straight-forward strategy emphasizing Brunswick's leadership positions and built on a solid foundation of basic values.

"Quality—we will either be the highest quality producer in every

market we serve or we won't be in that business," he wrote on one of those late nights.

To that he added: "Customers—we are in business to serve customers at a profit. Singularly, customer satisfaction is the most important responsibility we have to assure long-term success of the company."

And this: "People—of paramount importance is our people—their personal dignity, their pride in what they do, and the trust they have in their management."

"A lot of people don't understand numbers," Reichert said. "But everyone understands values."

And, with those values guiding Reichert's actions, Brunswick began to change.

The first priority after the disposition of Sherwood was the restructuring and streamlining of the company. The previous corporate structure was simply no longer suitable. "The pyramid was too tall and too cumbersome," Reichert said. "The levels of supervision had gotten so deep that it inhibited the sort of quick actions that were necessary."

He wanted everyone in on this process. "If you want to know how to do a job right," he said, "ask the person who is doing it."

Authority was delegated to the lowest levels at each division, with less interference from corporate staff. The positions of Chief Operating Officer and Group Executive were eliminated, cutting two tiers

The Zebco plant helps celebrate Reichert's birthday.

of management directly from the top of the organization.

Some of the actions Reichert took were immediately apparent. The company's eleven divisions were consolidated into eight. Space at the corporate offices was consolidated to one-third its previous size as staff was reduced. Two of the company's three jet aircraft were sold. The executive dining room was closed. In the process, some $20 million in annual corporate overhead vanished.

During this time, the makeup of the Board of Directors also changed when Jack Hanigan, John Rettaliata, Ian MacGregor, and Ed Stephan, having reached retirement age, left and Leo Herzel and Dr. Jay Lorsch were added.

During the next several months, the company divested four businesses not in leadership positions, and set about to fix those operations which were in need of fixing.

The Brunswick Division staff was relocated from the corporate offices in Skokie across Lake Michigan to Muskegon, Michigan, the site of its manufacturing facilities. By having management working more closely with manufacturing personnel, Reichert believed that operating costs could be reduced and more emphasis placed on the quality of goods being produced. One costly example of his desire to sell only high quality goods was the total recall of a bowling product which did not meet the standards set by the company.

Brunswick corporate headquarters in Skokie, a suburb north of Chicago.

"The warranty costs we had to absorb were enormous," he said. "But they were ones we had to incur in order to keep the trust of our customers."

Another of Reichert's plans took effect in mid-1982 with the establishment of the company's Venture Capital Program. Its internal board, consisting of James Urbanek, Senior Vice President of Administration; Henry Marvin, Vice President of Technology; Max McGrath, Vice President of Finance, and Bernard Kornhaber, Corporate Director of Planning, oversaw the allocation of corporate funds for the development of new technologies sponsored by a division. At the same time, efforts were stepped up to seek businesses which could be acquired to enhance the growth of the company's core businesses.

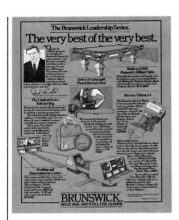

These national ads began appearing in 1983, emphasizing the tradition of quality in Brunswick's products.

Less than two years after taking over, Reichert could see his plans having a positive effect.

In less than two years after taking over as Brunswick's CEO—the title of Chairman was added in the fall of 1983 when Abernathy retired—Reichert could see the streamlining and emphasis on basic values having a positive effect on the bottom line and on the company's employees.

He cared about both. He made himself a visible boss, frequently visiting the company's far-flung facilities and stopping often to chat with the people working there. It was important to him that the more than 19,000 Brunswick employees feel a real part of the operation. He wanted their work to be a meaningful experience in which they could justifiably take pride.

"Jack wanted the employees to have dignity, feel pride in what they do and the company they work for," said William Niemann, Brunswick Vice President-Law,

Secretary and General Counsel, who ended his 26-year career with the company in 1985. "And, when the employees feel that way, as Jack points out, the numbers take care of themselves."

Reichert also believed that actions speak louder than words. And as 1983 drew to a close, he realized another goal—to make as many of the company's employees as possible shareholders in Brunswick.

"I always had a desire to make Brunswick employees instant capitalists and give them an immediate stake in the company's future," he said.

Toward that end, Reichert insisted that every employee get the same amount of stock regardless of their level or salary. The stock grant program was accomplished with the aid of the U.S. government's PAYSOP program which allows companies to receive a tax credit for the cost of the grant of stock to employees. But at Reichert's request, the Board added a bonus, matching the contribution covered under PAYSOP with a contribution right out of earnings.

"It was our people who were responsible for our strong performance in 1983, and this was a very visible way to demonstrate how much we appreciate these efforts," Reichert stated. "We also told them that, as long as the company's performance continued to grow, they would continue to benefit from the program." And so they did in 1984 as well.

Also, Reichert encouraged an increase in pension payouts to all pensioners. Historically, only former salaried employees receive such increases, but in 1984 the pension committee authorized inclusion of former hourly employees in the increased pension benefit.

With the revitalized commitment of its people and favorable economic conditions, Brunswick enjoyed record success. In 1983, company sales were $1.22 billion and its net earnings were $66.1 million, a record for earnings from continuing operations. Later that year, the company's common stock was split two-for-one in the form of a 100 percent stock dividend, the first such split since the bowling boom of the late 1950s.

"Of course, I was pleased," said Reichert. "I remember telling people in 1982 that my goal for the next year was to double the year's results. Nearly everyone told me it couldn't be done . . . well, they were right . . . with the help of a strong economy, we exceeded my goals by twenty percent."

And results in 1984 were better still: $1.47 billion in sales and $94.2 million in earnings. These numbers far surpassed the previous all time records of $1.34 billion in sales and $66.8 in earnings accomplished in 1981, while Sherwood was still a major contributor to the bottom line. As a result of the company's strong 1984 performance, the price of Brunswick

stock reached an all-time high early in 1985.

Shortly after those results were announced, one director seemed to speak for many Brunswick employees when he said, "Companies need to have a value system they can believe in. Jack spent a lot of time spreading his message, sharing his goals and expectations. And people believed. He had more than just some catchy phrases. He had the ability to make them realistic goals. And this company really went into high gear trying to attain them."

Brunswick stock reached an all-time high early in 1985. And Brunswick's employees shared in the gains.

15 *Brunswick Today*

The 116-year-old Brunswick-built library of Chicago's St. Ignatius College Prep would benefit from restoration funded by the Brunswick Foundation in 1985.

Whether a first time skier or a seasoned veteran, performance is the name of the skiing game. And Mercury performance is unbeatable.

There is no way to take a snapshot of Brunswick today that would allow people to see the total picture.

A corporation is an ever changing thing, at once firmly in the present, but at the same time a representation of its past and a glimpse of its future. This is true of Brunswick, its many parts, and its many people.

Brunswick today is Mercury Marine which, under the direction of its General Manager and Corporate Vice President, Richard Jordan, watched earnings soar in 1983 and 1984. Certainly an improved economy helped. But equally important were dramatic operational improvements in manufacturing, inventory management, and quality.

In 1983, the four divisions then existing under Mercury Marine—Mercury and Mariner outboard motors, MerCruiser stern drives and Quicksilver parts and accessories—were consolidated into one. Also that year, Mercury instituted its QUEST Program. An acronym for Quality by United Effort Secures Tomorrow, QUEST was conceived to address Mercury's international competitiveness through increased manufacturing efficiency and flexibility, the use of new tools such as "just-in-time" manufacturing techniques, statistical process control, continuous manufacturing process, and partnership relationships with suppliers.

Building on the legacy of Carl Kiekhaefer, Mercury had become

These current Mercury
employees continue
the tradition of quality
represented by this gold
medal awarded for the
company's production
in the 1800s.

the largest marine engine business in the world, with major facilities in Fond du Lac, Wisconsin; Stillwater, Oklahoma; St. Cloud, Florida; and Juarez, Mexico, with supporting facilities worldwide.

Brunswick is Zebco, which was able to drive down the cost of quality—rejects and external failures—by more than 76 percent in 1983. And more than doubled productivity in reel manufacturing between 1981 and 1984. In addition, to give something back to

the fishermen, it established the FishAmerica Foundation to fund the conservation and improvement of aquatic resources in the U.S. and Canada. In 1984, the division, headed by General Manager John Charvat, introduced its new line of Quantum baitcasting and spinning reels, a state-of-the-art line of fishing tackle.

In keeping with the strategy of building the company's core businesses through acquisitions, Zebco purchased the Motor Guide line of electric trolling motors manufactured in Starkville, Mississippi.

Brunswick is Brunswick Recreation Centers, the largest chain of retail bowling centers in the world. Under the direction of its General Manager, Arnold Fogel, this division reduced the number of its centers, most located in the U.S., Canada, and Europe, from 250 to about 170 by the summer of 1985. At the same time, modern centers were being built in rapidly expanding population areas. Between the fall of 1983 and the summer of 1985, six new centers opened in Florida, Arizona, and California markets. As well, the division undertook the modernization of its existing centers.

Brunswick is the Brunswick Division, the company's oldest operation, which manufactures capital equipment such as the innovative AS-80 Colorvision automatic scorer, bowling lanes, pinsetters, seating and locker units, and consumer products such as balls, bags, and shoes, as well

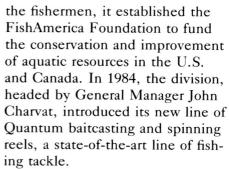

Zebco products working together: the new line of Quantum baitcasting reels and a Motor Guide electric trolling motor.

With Reichert at the forefront, Brunswick has been the leader in the effort to have bowling made an official Olympic sport.

as marketing Brunswick's classic line of billiard tables. Late in 1984, the division acquired Schmid & Company, a leading manufacturer of bowling equipment and supplies with operations in Switzerland and the Federal Republic of Germany.

In an effort to promote the image of bowling as a true international sport, Brunswick moved the company into a leadership position in an industry-wide effort to have bowling made an Olympic sport.

Brunswick is Defense. The company's largest technical operation, the Defense Division is headquartered in Skokie and headed by General Manager and Corporate Vice President Herbert Ennis. This division grew rapidly during the 1980s, eventually becoming the second largest in terms of sales

and earnings. Winning new contracts from the government and major subcontractors, the division built its backlog to record levels at the end of 1984 while setting records in sales and earnings.

It continued its leadership as the primary manufacturer of cam-

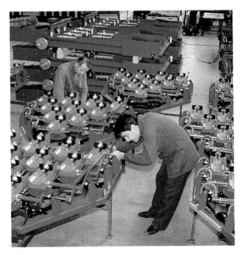

This revolutionary new pinsetting machine was among the products brought into the Brunswick fold with the 1984 acquisition of Schmid & Co.

135

From factory to action—radomes are extensively tested at the Defense Division's Marion, Virginia plant before riding the skies in aircraft such as the F-16.

Launch Rocket System was accomplished in 1984 in a new plant in Camden, Arkansas. Plant expansion was also undertaken at the division's joint venture, the Devil's Lake Sioux Manufacturing Corporation, in Devil's Lake, North Dakota, as it began production of new composite helmets for the Army. In 1985, as another example of overall corporate strategy, the division acquired the Advanced Technology Division of Deposition Technology, Inc., in San Diego, California.

Brunswick is Valve & Control, headquartered in Houston, Texas, and headed by General Manager Richard Wakenight. This division is comprised of Texsteam, in Houston, which produces valves, controls, and chemical injector pumps for the energy industry; GPE/RCS operation in Morton Grove, Illinois, which manufactures measuring and control devices for the energy and chemical process industries, and Circle Seal in Anaheim, California, which makes valves and controls for the aerospace, military, and industrial markets.

Valve & Control sponsored one of Brunswick's first Venture Capital Programs, an equity investment in Enhanced Energy System in Albuquerque, New Mexico, which manufactured direct contact steam generators used to facilitate the recovery of heavy oil. And late in 1984, the division acquired Cooper Resources & Energy, Inc., a leading maker of corrosion resistant

ouflage for the U.S. military. It also established itself as a major producer of mobile shelters, having won nearly $100 million in contracts for the Army Shelter Family in 1984, as well as other shelter programs for the Air Force and Marine Corps.

Such increases warranted the major expansion of the division's Marion, Virginia, facility. And the start up of its launch tube production for the U.S. Army's Multiple

136

valves for the petrochemical industry.

Brunswick is Technetics. This division is headquartered in DeLand, Florida, at one of its major manufacturing facilities, and is headed by General Manager Jack Singleton. The division is a leader in filtration technology with its Filterite product line, manufactured in Timonium, Maryland, and Fluid Dynamics, based in DeLand; and Wintec, based in Santa Ana, California.

Technetics has also been an active participant in the Venture Capital Program. A line of membrane filters used in high purification applications in the semi-conductor and health care industries was developed as was a new technology for the injection

molding of powdered metal parts. Another Technetics business is the production of golf club shafts produced in Torrington, Connecticut, under the Union Tubular Products name.

Brunswick is Vapor. This division, headquartered in Niles, Illinois, and run by General Manager William Parks, is a leading producer of components for the transportation industry such as door operators, environmental controls, relays and contactors. Orders for door operator systems for mass transit rail and bus projects continued strong in such markets as New York, Boston, Philadelphia and Atlanta, as well as for the new Metrorail system serving greater Miami. Vapor's plant in Montreal, Canada, continues to manufacture

Injection molding, being tested at the Technetics Division plant in Florida, is among Brunswick's newest technologies.

A workman inspects a Cooper valve, one of the new technologies acquired by the Valve & Control Division in 1984.

Large boilers are under construction at the Vapor Division plant in Sao Paulo, Brazil.

and sell similar products to growing mass transit and railroad markets in Canada. The division also made a major move to capture the growing market for electrical boilers in Brazil by establishing an assembly plant in Sao Paulo in 1983, and continues to explore new technologies such as sphere matrix heat exchangers as well as equipment to improve the fuel efficiency of diesel locomotives.

Brunswick is International. Over 1,750 Brunswick people today handle the manufacture, sales, distribution, and service of products in foreign markets. From Brunswick Recreation Centers in Canada, West Germany, and Austria, to Brunswick Division's Schmid operations in Switzerland and West Germany, to Mercury Marine manufacturing and assembly operations in Canada, Mexico, and Belgium, to Vapor facilities in

Canada and Brazil, to Brunswick's joint ventures with Mitsui (Nippon Brunswick) and Nireco (formerly Nihon Regulator Company) in Japan, and to the many divisional and corporate offices which support these operations, Brunswick is world-wide.

"It is amazing to watch the activity at all the divisions," said one division General Manager in the late summer of 1985. "Brunswick is . . . busy."

It is impossible, as Brunswick's 140-year story has vividly shown, to know what the future holds. But there is ample reason to believe, given its sturdy heritage and the rebirth of its adventurous spirit, that Brunswick will continue to succeed amid the world's unpredictable changes.

The products of Vapor Division are very visible on the mass transit systems of the world.

"We are a good company," Reichert said, sitting in his office late one afternoon in the summer of 1985. "But we still have a lot of work to do before we are excellent." On that day, he had just heard the news that the Brunswick Foundation had agreed to fund the restoration of the library at Chicago's St. Ignatius College Prep, a masterpiece in wood built by Brunswick craftsmen in 1872.

"That pleases me tremendously," Reichert said. "Have you seen it? It is magnificent. The craftsmanship. And more than a century old. There's no doubt about it. Quality lasts."

From the top of his desk he picked up a tiny valve and held it in his hand. It was a product from Valve & Control's Circle Seal operation, a small piece of metal that would have been of little interest to the untrained eye.

"Look at this," he said. "This valve was part of the Columbia Space Shuttle. This tiny thing has travelled a million and a half miles through space. Isn't that something?"

He paused for a moment and stared at the object.

"You know, it would be nice to be able to share the progress of this Company with John Brunswick. To show him this valve, talk to him about what we're doing, where we've been and where I think we're going," he said.

"I'd tell him how grateful I am for his risk-taking spirit, his value system, his concern for quality and

people. Thousands of others have contributed to what he started . . . changed it, expanded it. And, I'm proud of them all. Just think about it—one hundred and forty years ago the man planted a seed. And through good times and bad we've maintained our independence and built a strong company committed to a value system which will endure, to be built upon by those who follow."

One hundred and forty years old, Brunswick has an investment in America's future as its products soar into outer space.

Art and Photography Credits